THE GENESIS OF REVELATION

THE GENESIS

OF

REVELATION

SECRETS OF THE BIBLE REVEALED
AND A CASE FOR REFORMATION

THE JUDEO-CHRISTIAN EDITION

AERIK VONDENBURG

TWIN PILLARS PUBLISHING

Printed in the United States of America

Twin Pillars Publishing

Copyright 2011, 2017

Cover design by Trenor Rapkins.

Scripture taken from:

THE EXPANDED BIBLE. Copyright© 2011 by Thomas Nelson, Inc. Used by permission. All rights reserved.

GOD'S WORD®,©1995 God's Word to the Nations ("Names of God"). Used by Permission of Baker Publishing Group.

THE HOLY BIBLE, NEW INTERNATIONAL VERSION®, NIV® Copyright© 1973, 1978, 1984, 2011 by Biblica, Inc.® Used by permission. All rights reserved worldwide.

WORLD ENGLISH BIBLE. Public Domain.

ISBN-13: 978-0692900475

ISBN-10: 0692900470

CONTENTS

A NOTE FROM THE AUTHOR

Despite the controversial nature of the findings that are presented in this work, it is not my intention to denounce the primary principles of organized religion, nor any particular ethnic group. The information presented herein that does not conform to traditional Judeo-Christian doctrine pertains only to matters that are not related to the beneficial energy of the Holy Spirit, but with the mistaken interpretations of man.

—Aerik Vondenburg

For whatever is hidden is meant to be disclosed, and whatever is concealed is meant to be brought out into the open.

—Yeshua, Mark 4:22

PREFACE

The long journey that lead me into the research and writing of this book began in childhood. It was during those impressionable years that I was first told that the world, and all living things in it, had been created by God. I remember being perplexed by the concept of such an eternal being. If God exists, and if "he" created the universe, where then did God come from? And, if God once literally appeared in person in ancient times, why then does he not do so now? I eventually realized that I would never receive a credible answer to these childhood questions.

It was in my teenage years that I began to disassociate myself from my religious upbringing as I became more aware of the logical deductions of science. However, by the time that I was in my twenties I came to realize that mainstream scientists harbored their own dogmatic views. For example, I knew that the secular physicalist[1] bias that they held against subjects pertaining to the paranormal was unjustifiable after I personally experienced paranormal phenomena. The most stunning of which was the sighting of a luminescent anthropomorphic energy form. These experiences were, at least for myself, empirical evidence of what countless witnesses have been reporting for millennia. I therefore came to realize that just because mainstream scientists have not yet discovered a way to apprehend the anomalous aspects of nature does not mean that such phenomena does not exist.

The impetus that compelled me to research and write this book was a need for understanding. It was only after I released myself from the constricting influences of all forms of indoctrination that I was able to be receptive to more accurate deductions. My mentality during this life-altering quest was one of intrepid objectivity; and it is with this same type

---

1 Physicalism is a philosophy that asserts that all reality is confined to physical substance. It is a modern-age form of materialism. In this book, materialism refers to the interest in material items.

1

of clear and unbiased attitude that the following work should be approached.

What I eventually discovered is that the key to understanding could not only be found in the various scientific studies and historical texts of the world but in the discovery of the meaning of the "secrets" of the Bible.

* * *

This book is written from the perspective of a follower of the Judeo-Christian faith. It considers the defensible (i.e., moderate maximalist)[2] possibility that many of the events that are reported in the Bible, no matter how affected they may have become throughout the centuries, are at least generally based on actual people, places, and events, and that there are inexplicable forces at work in our world that scientists have yet to understand. Conversely, for the purpose of genuine inquiry, secular scholarly analysis will be examined and considered as well.

---

2 Biblical maximalists postulate that the events and characters in the Bible are, for the most part, true—as opposed to the minimalists, who believe that the Bible is a work of fiction.

PROLOGUE

THE books of the Bible have influenced the course of world events for millennia. Its stories and doctrines are familiar to even those who are not members of the religions of the Old and New Testaments. However, no other book is as misunderstood. What is especially unknown pertains to the "secret" matters that are referred to repeatedly throughout the scriptures.

> The secret things belong to the Lord our God; but the things revealed belong to us and to our children forever, that we may follow all the words of this law.
> —Deuteronomy 29:29

In the Old Testament, it is reported that the Lord God hid certain matters from humankind:

> It is the glory of God to conceal a matter [. . .]
> —Proverbs 25:2

> Oh, how I wish that God would speak, that he would open his lips against you and disclose to you the secrets of wisdom [. . .]
> —Job 11:5-6

God himself seems to confirm the existence of secrets in the following passage:

> Are you wiser than Daniel? Is no secret hidden from you?
> —Jehovah, Ezekiel 28:3

References to secret matters continue in the New Testament, where Jesus makes repeated references to hidden knowledge that was revealed only to his most trusted disciples:

> The knowledge of the secrets of the kingdom of God has been given to you, but to others I speak in parables [. . .]
> —Jesus, Luke 8:10

> If you, even you, had only known on this day what would bring you peace—but now it is hidden from your eyes.
> —Jesus, Luke 19:42

> The kingdom of heaven is like a treasure hidden in a field [. . .]
> —Jesus, Matthew 13:44

> [. . .] the knowledge of the secrets of the kingdom of heaven has been given to you, but not to them.
> —Jesus, Matthew 13:11

> For whatever is hidden is meant to be disclosed, and whatever is concealed is meant to be brought out into the open.
> —Jesus, Mark 4:22

Because the secret matters have either been relegated to the status of the forbidden, or assumed to exist outside the range of human comprehension, they have never been fully disclosed and understood.

4

However, clues left to us in the ancient records, including the Bible itself, have made it possible to uncover these hidden matters for the first time in the present age. The secrets will reveal that almost everything that is commonly understood about biblical history and its tenets has been based upon an astonishing misunderstanding.

CHAPTER I

THE THEOCRACY OF
YAHWEH

Historic changes were taking place in Mesopotamia in around the second millennium BCE, as the old city-states of Sumer and Akkad declined and Assyria and Babylonia arose up in their place. It was during that era—or perhaps not long after—that a mysterious deity made his presence known in that region. A being who made the intrepid claim that he was the supreme God of all the heavens and Earth. A being who referred to himself by the enigmatic maxim, "I am who I am" (*Eyeh asher eyeh*); which later came to be translated as Yahweh.[3]

Unlike the other gods of the age, no specific visual images of this deity were depicted in the official artworks of his followers.[4] Although Yahweh was described as having a physical body, he was also represented in the amorphous forms of smoke, clouds, and fire as well. Not only did Yahweh mysteriously appear in the physical world of man but also disappeared in an equally enigmatic manner, never to be known in such

---

3 The designation "Yahweh" is derived from the abbreviated four root consonant letters YHWH. In Hebrew, these letters denote: being, becoming, creation, and existence.

4 The drachm coin of Yehud (fourth century BC), which depicts a bearded man on a winged and wheeled throne (which is similar to the Ezekiel description) with the Aramaic letters YHW, or YHD, next to it, is a possible exception (British Museum. Registration number: TC,p242.5.Pop). However, even though the coin was minted in Judah, it was issued by a Persian administration and shows signs of Greek influence.

6

direct and physical terms ever again.

Who then exactly was this mysterious individual who came to be known to the world as "God"?

According to the biblical record, the era of the theocracy of Yahweh began in earnest when a man from the Sumero-Akkadian city of Ur was contacted by an anonymous deity who engaged him in a covenant that would give birth to a new society in the Near East.[5] This man is referred to in the Bible as Abram/Abraham, and the nameless individual who contacted him eventually came to be known as "Yahweh"; although, this was not the name that Abraham knew him as:

> [. . .] I am Yahweh; and I appeared to Abraham, to Isaac, and to Jacob as God Almighty [El Shaddai]; but by my name Yahweh I was not known to them.
> —Yahweh, Exodus 6:2-3

It seems that he did not begin to be addressed as Yahweh until the time of Moses:

> God [Elohim] said to Moses, "I AM WHO I AM. This is what you are to say to the Israelites: 'I AM [*Ehyeh*] has sent me to you.' " God also said to Moses, "Say to the Israelites, 'The Lord [Yahweh], the God of your fathers—the God of Abraham, the God of Isaac and the God of Jacob—has sent me to you.' This is my name forever, the name that you shall call me from generation to generation."
> —Yahweh, Exodus 3:14-15

However, according to Genesis 4:1 God was called Yahweh since the time of Adam and Eve. However, scholars now know that this designation was inserted by a Yahwist (i.e., J source)[6] scribe at a later time.

---

5 This edition will focus primarily on the deity who referred to himself as the "God of Abraham, the God of Isaac, and the God of Jacob" (Exodus 3:6); as opposed to the "Elohim" of the earlier Genesis account. This difference will be studied more closely in the Esoteric Edition.

6 According to the prevailing Documentary Hypothesis, one of the four primary

According to custom, the name of God (the *Tetragrammaton*) is considered to be too sacred to speak aloud; therefore, he is instead usually addressed by other designations, such as Adonai (Lord) or Ha-El (the true God).

Yahweh would rarely appear to the people in public, and when he did it was usually from behind some type of fiery or smoky obstruction (e.g., Deuteronomy 4:15). In this case, the question must be asked: Could the obscuration of his identity have anything to do with the secret hidden matters of God?

The biblical record tells us that Yahweh was known to purposely hide his face from the children of Israel:

> O Yahweh [. . .] when you hid your face I was terrified.
> —Psalm 30:7

> Truly you are a God who has been hiding himself [. . .]
> —Isaiah 45:15

> Neither will I hide my face any more from them; for I have poured out my Spirit on the house of Israel.
> —Yahweh, Ezekiel 39:29

Although some of these instances could be interpreted to mean that Yahweh had turned his back upon the disobedient people, when these reports are put into context with other biblical passages another reason for his mysterious disappearances begins to emerge. Consider the following passage, for example, in which Yahweh is specifically described hiding his face, as opposed to turning his back upon a disobedient people. In the account that is recorded in the book of Exodus, Moses asked Yahweh to let him see his face. Yahweh refused; although he did allow Moses to see his back as he walked away:

> Then the Lord said, "There is a place near me where you

---

authors of the first five books of the Bible (i.e., the Torah) was a scribe from the southern kingdom of Judah, circa eighth century BC, who referred to God as YHWH.

8

may stand on a rock. When my glory passes by, I will put you in a cleft in the rock and cover you with my hand until I have passed by. Then I will remove my hand and you will see my back; but my face must not be seen."
—Yahweh, Exodus 33:21-23

Therefore, it is possible that when Moses met with Yahweh "face to face" (Deuteronomy 34:10), this was either the scribe's way of saying in person, or Yahweh eventually changed his mind, or this is a contradiction.

Why then did Yahweh make such an effort to obscure himself? In order to answer this question, it is necessary to understand his motivation.

* * *

The biblical record indicates that it was Yahweh's desire to establish an empire in the land of Canaan. In order to do this, he employed various governing techniques; some of which involved the use of clandestine operations. In these accounts, Yahweh is reported using different opposing kingdoms that were each under his control in order to inflict punishment on one another. Only by swearing allegiance to him could the people expect to be spared the onslaught of one of his armies.

Yahweh will bring against you a nation from far away, from the ends of the earth. The nation will swoop down on you like an eagle [. . .]
—Deuteronomy 28:49

I will use them [the Philistines, Canaanites, etc.] to test Israel and see whether they will keep the way of the Lord and walk in it as their ancestors did.
—Yahweh, Judges 2:22

When the troublesome King Manasseh kept "seducing" Judah and the inhabitants of Jerusalem by causing them to stray from servitude to the Lord (2 Chronicles 33), Yahweh retaliated by ordering the Assyrians to attack and capture the offender and exile him to Babylon—which was yet another city-state that was under his control at that time. Manasseh was released from incarceration only after he reaffirmed his allegiance to Yahweh.

An explanation for this type of activity comes to us from the sixteenth-century Italian political philosopher, Niccolo Machiavelli. In his books *The Prince* and *The Discourses on Livy*, Machiavelli proposed ways for a ruler to acquire and secure power for himself. He recommended the employment of strategic operations that would serve to control a populace. Examples of what Machiavelli described are not only found in the Old Testament but they are found repeatedly. In the book of Deuteronomy, for example, it is reported that Yahweh threatened those who did not obey him with "calamities" and "distress":

> Then my anger shall be kindled against them in that day, and I will forsake them, and I will hide my face from them, and they shall be devoured, and many evils and troubles shall come on them; so that they will say on that day, 'Haven't these evils come on us because our God is not among us?'
> —Yahweh, Deuteronomy 31:17

What the people did not always know is that many of the calamities that they were experiencing were brought upon them by Yahweh himself. It was an operation that was designed to convince the people that servitude to himself was in their own best interest. When his people abandoned him by not submitting themselves as workers, warriors, and worshipers, he would in turn abandon them to their enemies—enemy forces that were often, if not always, under his control as well. Of course, this was also a technique that could be reversed if needed, in order to keep the other in line as well.

Another territory that was of interest to Yahweh was Egypt. In the following passage, Yahweh discloses that he will conquer the Egyptians by dividing it against itself—which compares to the Machiavellian strategy of subjugation through division:

10

> And I will stir up the Egyptians against Egyptians, and they will fight everyone against his brothers, and everyone against his neighbor; city against city, kingdom against kingdom.
> —Yahweh, Isaiah 19:2

> Yahweh has mixed a spirit of perverseness in the middle of her; and they have caused Egypt to go astray in all of its works, like a drunken man staggers in his vomit.
> —Isaiah 19:14

This state of bewilderment was how Yahweh was not only able to dominate his enemies and subdue the disobedient among his own army but produce a state of unrest that only he himself could provide relief from.

> Yahweh will send you curses, panic, and frustration in everything you do until you're destroyed and quickly disappear for the evil you will do by abandoning Yahweh.
> —Deuteronomy 28:20

Besides using opposing forces to keep one another in check, he also purposely endeavored to produce a state of confusion and fear, which he was also able to use to his advantage:

> Better to have a little with the fear of Yahweh than great treasure and turmoil.
> —Proverbs 15:16

Indeed, the instigation of fear was recommended by Machiavelli:

> Men are moved by two principle things—by love and by fear. Consequently, they are commanded as well by someone who wins their affection as by someone who arouses

11

their fear. Indeed in most instances the one that arouses their fear gains more of a following and is more readily obeyed than the one who wins their affection.
—Machiavelli, *Discourses on Livy*

[. . .] The fear of Yahweh is your treasure.
—Isaiah 33:6

This is why the followers of Yahweh refer to themselves as the "God fearing":

Serve Yahweh with fear, and rejoice with trembling.
—Psalm 2:11

Of course, fear is the emotion that relates with not only confusion but with violence:

It will happen in that day, that a great panic from Yahweh will be among them; and they will lay hold everyone on the hand of his neighbor, and his hand will rise up against the hand of his neighbor.
—Zechariah 14:13

Indeed, the threat of violence was a strong motivational force that Yahweh was also able to use to his advantage:

I sent plagues among you like I did to Egypt. I have slain your young men with the sword, and have carried away your horses; and I filled your nostrils with the stench of your camp, yet you haven't returned to me.
—Yahweh, Amos 4:10

If the people felt that they did not have a reason to be in need of a benefactor, Yahweh would provide one for them by sending an opposing army that was also under his control to frighten them into submission.

Once they had been sufficiently intimidated, he would then arrive to present himself as their guardian benefactor and vanquish the enemy threat. The catch was that they were then indebted to him as their liberator.

In order to preserve the clandestine nature of those operations, a certain amount of secrecy was necessary in order to keep those who were involved from knowing that they were being "deceived":

> I said, "Lord Yahweh, you certainly have deceived these
> people and Jerusalem" [. . .]
> —Jeremiah 4:10

> O Yahweh, you deceived me, and I was deceived [. . .]
> —Jeremiah 20:7

Some proponents of the traditional interpretation of these passages, and the translators who are influenced by them, will sometimes euphemize the word for "deceive" (New International Version translation; English Standard translation), or "fooled" (New World translation), or "misled" (New Living translation), by instead translating the word as "persuaded" (King James translation), or even "enticed" (New Revised Standard translation). However, these softer definitions do not correspond with the original context of the Machiavellian operations that were occurring at that time.

In the following passage, Yahweh is recorded soliciting the help of a deceptive spirit who will help deceive his enemies:

> Yahweh asked, "Who will deceive Ahab so that he will
> attack and be killed at Ramoth in Gilead?" Some answered
> one way, while others said something else. Then Ruach [a
> spirit] stepped forward, stood in front of Yahweh, and said,
> "I will deceive him." "How?" Yahweh asked. Ruach
> answered, "I will go out and be a spirit that tells lies
> through the mouths of all of Ahab's prophets." Yahweh
> said, "You will succeed in deceiving him. Go and do it."

13

So, Yahweh has put into the mouths of all these prophets of yours a spirit that makes them tell lies. Yahweh has spoken evil about you.

—1 Kings 22:20-23

It is therefore evident that Yahweh's plan did not involve diplomatic "enticing," but rather the deliberate implementation of operations that were intended to both "deceive" and to "confuse."

Be ever hearing, but never understanding; be ever seeing, but never perceiving. Make the heart of this people calloused; make their ears dull and close their eyes. Otherwise they might see with their eyes, hear with their ears, understand with their hearts. And turn and be healed.

—Yahweh, Isaiah 6:9-10

Yahweh has poured out on you a spirit of deep sleep. He will shut your eyes (your eyes are the prophets) [. . .]

—Isaiah 29:10

It was essential that the people who he sought to control were not entirely aware of his full intentions and capabilities. By concealing himself, and by consorting with the other nations that were also under his control, he was better able to control those who did not know who or what they were dealing with.

Why are you so distant, Yahweh? Why do you hide yourself in times of trouble?

—Psalms 10:1

Indeed, according to Numbers 22 Yahweh did personally engage with a high-ranking member of another nation behind the scenes when he met with a non-Israelite man named Balaam, who agreed to help Yahweh by refusing to help the Moabites.

14

* * *

Babylon was sacked by the Assyrian king Sennacherib in 689 BCE. This is the same king who ordered his men to march against Jerusalem. In the biblical account, it is reported that Sennacherib had been ordered to attack Jerusalem by Yahweh himself. This was supposedly done because the Judeans had formed an unauthorized alliance with Egypt (2 Kings 18:13-25). A similar fate had befallen the northern kingdom of Israel years earlier, after they had not followed the "commandments of Moses" (2 Kings 18:9-12).

Despite the usefulness that the Assyrian super-power provided him, they too eventually fell out of favor with Yahweh. After King Hezekiah renewed his allegiance, Yahweh put an end to the Assyrian threat by ordering an angel to destroy their camp in the middle of the night.[7] According to Isaiah 45:1, Cyrus, the king of Achaemenid Persia, was also under the guidance of Yahweh. Apparently, Yahweh even referred to Cyrus as his "anointed" one (i.e., Messiah). Here we find another example of Yahweh using foreign kings that were also under his control. In Ezra 1:1 (and 2 Chronicles 36:22), it is reported that Cyrus, "in order to fulfill the word of the Lord spoken by Jeremiah," proclaimed that the Lord God had told him to build a temple in Jerusalem. The book of Jeremiah makes it very clear that it was Yahweh's plan for the kingdom of Judah to fall to the Babylonians. After the Judeans had been sufficiently terrorized into submission and prayed for help, Yahweh then commenced with the second phase of his plan; namely, to destroy the Babylonians who had attacked the holy city of Jerusalem (Jeremiah 51:24); after which he was then able to present himself as the almighty savior of the people.

> Babylon was a golden cup in Yahweh's hand.
> —Jeremiah 51:7

When the people began to suspect that they were being manipulated, Yahweh admonished them:

---

7 According to the Assyrian prism annals, this event did not occur.

15

Do not call conspiracy everything this people calls a conspiracy [. . .]
—Yahweh, Isaiah 8:12

What is conspicuous about this passage is that Yahweh denies that there is a conspiracy, while in the very same breath (Isaiah 8:14) he admits that he has set a "trap and a snare" for the people of Jerusalem! This section of the book of Isaiah ends with the author stating that he will wait for "the Lord who is hiding his face from the house of Jacob." Therefore, it is evident that Yahweh was not simply turning his back upon the disobedient people, but rather was also turning away in order to carry out his Machiavellian operations.

Yahweh has accomplished what he had planned to do. He carried out the threat he announced long ago. He tore you down without any pity, Jerusalem. He made your enemies gloat over you. He raised the weapons of your opponents.
—Lamentations 2:17

Likewise, in the following passage Yahweh is described as the one who makes "plans" to rule over the people:

Yahweh foils the plans of the nations; he thwarts the purpose of the peoples. But the plans of Yahweh stand firm forever [. . .]
—Psalm 33:10-11

It is evident that the story of Yahweh was a source of inspiration for Machiavelli, who did indeed refer to the Bible:

Therefore, it was needful that Moses find the people of Israel enslaved and oppressed by the Egyptians in order that they would be ready to follow him out of Egypt to escape from servitude.

16

—Niccolo Machiavelli, *The Prince*

* * *

In order to bring about his theocracy, Yahweh required workers, warriors, and worshipers. One of the problems that he had to contend with was independently-minded people who were not interested in submitting themselves as his servants:

> He [Yahweh] does not regard any who are wise of heart.
> —Job 37:24

> A loner is out to get what he wants for himself. He opposes
> all sound reasoning.
> —Proverbs 18:1

Yahweh and his retinue of priests, prophets, and scribes, constructed a doctrine in which the "wise" are those who are obedient, while the "stupid" are those who are "self-confident"—which was also equated with evil and sin (Proverbs 14:16).

In the book of Ezekiel, we are told that the king of Tyre had aroused the wrath of Yahweh by independently acquiring "gold" and "wisdom." His punishment was destruction by the army of the Lord:

> Because you think you are wise, as wise as a god, I am
> going to bring foreigners against you, the most ruthless of
> nations; they will draw their swords against your beauty
> and wisdom and pierce your shining splendor.
> —Yahweh, Ezekiel 28:6-7

The self-described "jealous God" (Exodus 20.5) condemned those who were driven by their own personal ambitions.

One of the ways that he was able to inflict punishment and assert his will was by the use of Machiavellian operations.[8] This is one of the

---

8 If the Machiavellian theory is correct, then there should be some mention of Yahweh

secrets of Yahweh; although, it was not the only one. The scriptures indicate that there was more going on than only Machiavellian operations.

* * *

In the King James Bible, the epithet of Yahweh is translated as "Lord of hosts." The word hosts is commonly interpreted as an assembly of angels; however, this is not the original definition. This term derives from the original Hebrew root word *sabat* (i.e., *sabaoth*), which literally means armies. This is a definition that accurately relates to the activities and characteristics of Yahweh. Indeed, this rendering is used in several translations of the Bible (e.g., New Translations Bible; God's Word Translation; World English Bible):

> Yahweh of Armies has planned it, to stain the pride of all
> glory, to bring into contempt all the honorable of the earth.
> —Isaiah 23:9

Indeed, the biblical record tells us that Yahweh was an almighty lord of war:

> Cursed are those who neglect doing Yahweh's work.
> Cursed are those who keep their swords from killing.
> —Yahweh, Jeremiah 48:10

> The dead bodies of men shall fall as dung on the open field
> [. . .]
> —Yahweh, Jeremiah 9:22

> Yahweh is a man of war. Yahweh is his name.
> —Exodus 15:3

---

in the records of the foreign nations that he conspired with. I contend that these records do exist. This subject will be examined in the Esoteric Edition of this work.

18

In a few biblical translations, the name and title Yahweh of Armies is translated as "Lord Almighty" (e.g., Isaiah 13:4-5, 13:13) (The Living Bible; New International Version), despite the fact that there is no justifiable reason for these words to appear. The original Hebrew words *Yahweh Sabaoth* does not mean "Lord Almighty." This is a misleading misnomer that has been devised by well-meaning translators who have euphemized the literal definition in order to make it more palatable to the laity.

The truth is that the Old Testament is filled with examples of Yahweh inflicting both his enemies as well as his own people with the weapons of his "arsenal" (Jeremiah 50:25). Whenever he felt that the people were not properly serving him, he would in turn inflict them with what we would refer to today as "weapons of mass destruction." His arsenal included both fiery projectiles as well as biological affliction in the form of disease. In some cases, he would even instruct those closest to him to conduct mass executions. Indeed, the military campaigns and carnage of the Lord of Armies is found all throughout the Old Testament:

> By the wrath of Yahweh of Armies the land will be scorched and the people will be fuel for the fire [. . .]
> —Isaiah 9:19

> Those destined for death, to death; those for the sword, to the sword; those for starvation, to starvation; those for captivity, to captivity.
> —Yahweh, Jeremiah 15:2

> I will execute judgment on him with plague and bloodshed [. . .]
> —Yahweh, Ezekiel 38:22

> Everyone who is found will be thrust through. Everyone who is captured will fall by the sword. Their infants also will be dashed to pieces before their eyes. Their houses will be ransacked, and their wives raped.

—Yahweh, Isaiah 13:15-16

Slaughter the old men, the young men and women, the
mothers and children [. . .]
—Yahweh, Ezekiel 9:6

Those who managed to survive the onslaught were taken into captivity as
slaves, like a herd of cattle:

[. . .] I will put my hook in your nose and my bit in your
mouth, and I will make you return by the way you came.
—Yahweh, 2 Kings 19:28

Yahweh demanded that ceremonial offerings be brought to him, and if
those offerings were not to his liking, or not carried out in a precise way
—such as in the case of the two sons of Aaron (Leviticus 10)—he would
show his displeasure by burning the offenders to death. It seems that no
one suffered under the leadership of Yahweh more than his own people:

Yahweh will cause you to be defeated before your enemies
[. . .] Your carcasses will be food for all the birds of the air
and wild animals [. . .] Yahweh will afflict you with the
boils of Egypt and with tumors, festering sores and the itch,
from which you cannot be cured. Yahweh will afflict you
with madness, blindness and confusion of mind.
—Deuteronomy 28:25-28

Part of the Machiavellian plan was to continually remind the people that
they were indebted to him for liberating them from enslavement in Egypt.
When the people began to realize that they were out of the frying pan and
into the fire, so to speak, they began to wish that they had never left
Egypt. Indeed, a little-known part of this popular story is that at a later
time some of the people actually returned to Egypt! Therefore, it can be
concluded that the reason why the Judean-Israelites were continually
turning toward other gods was because they may have felt that they were

20

in need of protection from Yahweh himself! When Yahweh found out that some of the people had returned to Egypt, he declared that just because they had fled from him did not mean that they would be safe from his wrath:

> Woe to the obstinate children [. . .] who go down to Egypt without consulting me; who look for help to Pharaoh's protection, to Egypt's shade for refuge.
> —Yahweh, Isaiah 30:1-2

> 'I swear by my great name,' says Yahweh, 'that no one from Judah living anywhere in Egypt will ever again invoke my name or swear, "As surely as Lord Yahweh lives." For I am watching over them for harm, not for good; the Jews in Egypt will perish by sword and famine until they are all destroyed.
> —Yahweh, Jeremiah 44:26-27

Although it is known that Yahweh was a "jealous" "fire and brimstone" type of character, what is less commonly understood is the full extent of his actions. For example, the biblical record tells us that Yahweh sentenced those who did not submit to him to terrible, humiliating, and agonizing punishments and deaths:

> I am going to punish your descendants. I am going to spread excrement on your faces, the excrement from your festival sacrifices. You will be discarded with it.
> —Yahweh, Malachi 2:3

The enemies of the Lord who escaped death were sometimes sentenced to slavery. Indeed, slavery was a practice that Yahweh permitted:

> You may have male and female slaves, but buy them from the nations around you.
> —Yahweh, Leviticus 25:44

21

Yahweh was not only interested in physical slavery but mental subjugation as well. In the system that Yahweh and his agents established, righteousness and wisdom were equated with obedience, while disobedience was equated with sin and foolishness:

> The wise in heart accept commands, but a chattering fool comes to ruin.
> —Proverbs 10:8

Anyone who was able to perceive and formulate judgments based on their own reasoning were subjected to ridicule, threats, and violent punishments:

> Woe to those who are wise in their own eyes and clever in their own sight.
> —Isaiah 5:21

By keeping his subjects unaware, Yahweh was better able to fuse the affairs of church and state, and thereby create a reliable and effective warrior class who were willing to give up their lives for the campaign. Indeed, fusing the affairs of church and state was a practice that was recommended by Machiavelli[9] when he praised the "leaders and founders of religions," who together with the "founders of republics and kingdoms," and the "commanders of armies," "extend the boundaries of their kingdom or country."

The purpose of bestowing the Ten Commandments was so that Yahweh could establish a functioning society, and thus a functioning army. Likewise, when he told the people to "be fruitful and multiply" (Genesis 26:4; Leviticus 26:9), this was not so much of a patriarchal benediction, but rather he simply needed to increase the population of his army! By establishing a code of law, he was better able to reduce internal strife among the people and keep them united and focused on the goal of accomplishing his desires.

The record indicates that Yahweh not only had an aberrant interest in

---

9 *Discourses on Livy*

power and worldly prestige but in material affluence as well. For example, he demanded that "gold, silver, and bronze" (as well as other treasures) be captured and added to his treasure trove:

> All the silver and gold and everything made of bronze and iron are holy and belong to Yahweh. They must go into Yahweh's treasury.
> —Joshua 6:19

> The silver is mine and the gold is mine, declares Yahweh of Armies.
> —Haggai 2:8

Those who submitted themselves as workers, warriors, and worshipers, were used for this purpose; while those who refused were put to death.

Some of those who did the bidding of the Lord were rewarded for their obedience with the material spoils of conquest:

> I will give you the treasures of darkness, and hidden riches of secret places [. . .]
> —Yahweh, Isaiah 45:3

> The Babylonians will become the prize. All who loot them will get everything they want.
> —Yahweh, Jeremiah 50:10

In Joshua 7, we are told that a man, who is referred to as Achan, was caught taking plundered treasure that was supposed to be offered to Yahweh. After Joshua was made aware of this transgression, he ordered that Achan be stoned to death.

Yahweh's campaign not only involved the acquisition of wealth but of also attaining the prime strategic land of Canaan as well. This acquisition would then lead to even more wealth and power, due to the fact that it was a region that was situated in between the western Mediterranean Sea civilizations and the eastern lands of Mesopotamia and Asia, which made it an important and strategic location. In fact, the ancient Hebrew word for merchant (*Kena'ani*) was used to describe a person from Canaan.[1]

> You have expanded the nation, O Yahweh. You have expanded the nation. You are honored. You have extended all the land's boundaries
> —Isaiah 26:15

Yahweh was clearly not only interested in acquiring land and wealth but needed to have his ego appeased as well. This was not something that he wished for; this was something that he demanded:

> Honor Yahweh your God before it gets dark, before your feet stumble on the mountains in the twilight. You will look for light, but Yahweh will turn it into the shadow of death and change it into deep darkness.
> —Jeremiah 13:16

At the very core of his motivation was a deep desire to be exalted as the "Most High" "Lord Almighty":

> I will be exalted among the nations, I will be exalted in the earth.
> —Yahweh, Psalm 46:10

* * *

According to the Old Testament/Tanakh itself, Yahweh was a deity who resided in a dark and fiery netherworld:

> Clouds and darkness surround him. Righteousness and justice are the foundations of his throne. Fire spreads out ahead of him. It burns his enemies who surround him. His flashes of lightning lights up the world. The earth sees them and trembles.

24

—Psalm 97:2-4

Will not the day of Yahweh be darkness, and not light; and will it not have been gloom, and not brightness? I have hated, I have rejected your festivals, and I shall not enjoy the smell of your solemn assemblies.
—Yahweh, Amos 5:20-21

Yahweh has said that he would dwell in the thick darkness.
—1 Kings 8:12

In Isaiah 6:1, we are informed that Lord Yahweh was seen seated upon a throne in a smoke-filled temple, surrounded by bizarre half-man half-beasts who are referred to as the "seraphim." In this scene, Yahweh orders Isaiah to go forth and "dull" the hearts and minds of the people (Isaiah 6:10).

According to the Old Testament/Tanakh itself, Yahweh was not only "deceiving" the people but was afflicting them with "terrible" "adversity":

Terror and pit and snare await you, people of the earth. Whosoever flees at the sound of terror will fall into a pit; whosoever climbs out of the pit will be caught in a snare [. . .] In that day Yahweh will punish the powers in the heavens above and the kings on the earth below.
—Isaiah 24:17-21

Lord Yahweh of Armies has a day of tumult and trampling and terror in the Valley of Vision [. . .]
—Isaiah 22:5

Although the Lord gives you the bread of adversity and the water of affliction, your teachers will be hidden no more [. . .].
—Isaiah 30:20

I trampled the nations in my anger; in my wrath I made them drunk and poured their blood on the ground.
—Yahweh, Isaiah 63:6

I will gather all the nations to Jerusalem to fight against it; the city will be captured, the houses ransacked, and the woman raped [. . .]
—Yahweh, Zechariah 14:2

Their infants also will be dashed in pieces before their eyes. Their houses will be ransacked, and their wives raped.
—Yahweh, Isaiah 13:16

These references to the killing of infants brings up other questions that pertain to child sacrifice, which was a practice that was not unheard of in the ancient Near East. Indeed, it is mentioned numerous times in the Old Testament/Tanakh. It is commonly believed that Yahweh condemned this practice, which is confirmed several times (e.g., Leviticus 20:2; Jeremiah 7:31, etc.). However, other verses contradict these decrees. For example, the following passage references Topheth. This was supposedly a location where the wicked heathens sacrificed their children to the foreign gods, such as Moloch (i.e., Molek) (Leviticus 18:21; 2 Kings 23:10). However, other biblical verses indicate that Yahweh did condone such practices when they were committed under his order. Indeed, the following verse indicates that it was Yahweh himself who ignited the sacrificial flame at Topheth:

Topheth has long been prepared; it has been made ready for the king. Its fire pit has been made deep and wide, with an abundance of fire and wood; the breath of the Lord, like a stream of burning sulfur, sets it ablaze.
—Isaiah 30:33

26

It is true that this verse indicates that it was the king of Assyria who was destined for the sacrificial flame at Topheth. However, the following verse reports that, at least at one time, Yahweh had forced the Israelites themselves to sacrifice their children as a punishment for their disobedience:

> So I gave them other statutes that were not good and laws through which they could not live; I defiled them [the people of Israel] through their gifts—the sacrifice of every firstborn—that I might fill them with horror so they would know that I am the Lord.
> —Yahweh, Ezekiel 20:25-26

The biblical record itself confirms that it was Yahweh who burned with an angry hatred in the gloomy darkness. It was Yahweh who devised deceptive schemes that were intended to gain power and egotistical glory for himself at the expense of innocent people. It was Yahweh who commanded his servants to perform blood-spilling rituals. It was Yahweh who ordered his troops to dismember children and rape woman. Although these are all characteristics that are usually associated with the devil, evil, and Satanism, the biblical record reports that it was Yahweh and his associates who were responsible for this behavior!

The reason why Yahweh went to such great lengths to conceal his true identity was not only related to his clandestine Machiavellian operations but also because he was not who he said that he was. The fire, smoke, and whirlwinds, were all a part of a fantastic facade that was used to convey a God-like supernatural power.

Although it is well known in the Judeo-Christian tradition that the devil is a malicious deceiver, what nobody considered is that the deception could have already happened.

> O Yahweh, you deceived me, and I was deceived [. . .]
> —Jeremiah 20:7

The individual who became known as "Yahweh" is the fallen arch-

angel who rebelled against the higher natural spirit of the universe. He is the infamous outlaw who arrogantly dared to assume the role of the Creator. He is the rebel whose soul burned with hatred, jealousy, and the deepest and most terrifying anger. He is the war criminal who used violence, deception, and fear to achieve personal power, wealth, and egotistical fame. The ultimate secret of Yahweh is that he himself fits the description of the devil character.

* * *

Of course, it is commonly assumed that Yahweh was a just and righteous "God"; a God of compassion and mercy. In this case, is there anything in the Old Testament that indicates that this is true? In the book of Zechariah, Yahweh is reported uttering the following statement:

> I will strengthen the people of Judah. I will rescue Joseph's people. I will bring them back, because I have compassion for them.
> —Yahweh, Zechariah 10:6

Likewise, in the following passage a devotee makes a reference to the Lord's love:

> Return, Yahweh. Deliver my soul, and save me for your loving kindness' sake.
> —Psalm 6:4

When conditions permitted, Yahweh seemed to make an effort to be gracious and merciful; however, these conditional gestures were only a temporary reward for behavior that conformed to his scheme. Only those who fell into line under the oppressive regulations of his machinations were granted clemency from his cruelty. For example, in Exodus 34:6-7 it is reported that the Lord declared his abounding "love"—that is, for those who he did not have to violently punish for not submitting themselves as workers, warriors, and worshipers. In these cases, the benevolent side that he occasionally displayed acted as more of a baiting device that led optimistic followers deeper into the deceptive spell that he and his collaborators were casting.

Over the course of time, misunderstanding increased as mistaken interpretation and affected information replaced personal experience and sensible reason. The more that time passed, the more these misunderstandings became familiar, aggrandized, sanitized, and absolute.

Imagine, for instance, if people were presented with a picture of an individual who was filled with burning rage, bitter jealousy, and violent outbursts. A deceptive schemer who commanded the people to bow beneath him or else suffer a cruel and agonizing death. A sociopathic tyrant who ordered his troops to intentionally kill children and rape woman. Such an individual would be regarded as not only a despot but as downright evil; and yet, this is not how Yahweh is commonly perceived. This situation is a testament to the influential power of the conditioning of mental perspective.

> Yahweh will afflict you with madness, and blindness, and confusion of mind.
> —Deuteronomy 28:28

Lay people are generally influenced by what appeals to them on more of an emotional level. The hardened traditionalists who promote and preserve the mistaken interpretation are able to dispel the negative aspects by redirecting focus away from the atrocities and the contradictions, and instead place attention onto matters that are related to the heart. However, it must be remembered that Yahweh and his original cohorts were not always advocates of the heart.

> The heart is deceitful above all things, and it is exceedingly corrupt: who can know it?
> —Yahweh, Jeremiah 17:9

Although Yahweh is given credit with bestowing the moral standard of the Ten Commandments, what must be understood is that the reason why he required law and order was simply because he needed a functioning servant force. What is also not so well known is that Yahweh was guilty of breaking most of those very laws himself! He was a murderer who coveted and stole and bore false testimony in order to carry out his materialistic and malevolent schemes.

In the biblical New Testament (Galatians 5.19-21), we read that the apostle Paul, who himself was a devout follower of Yahweh, lists the sins that will not allow a person to enter heaven. Among these infractions are "immorality, impurity, enmity, strife, jealousy, anger, selfishness," and "dissension." Of course, what Paul failed to realize is that Yahweh was guilty of committing those very sins himself! Yahweh was also guilty of committing most of the Seven Deadly Sins (as formulated by the Christian monk Evagrius of Pontus, and amended by Pope Gregory in the sixth century AD). These transgressions include: pride, envy, anger, and greed.

Some committed Judeo-Christian apologists have attempted to excuse the contradictions and the atrocities by asserting that "God must sometimes use evil to defeat evil." If this is the case, then there is no such thing as any moral standard because hypocrisy and heinous acts could always be justified as long as it fit someone's own idea of right and wrong. However, a double-standard is a double-standard, no matter who it is that is the hypocrite.

* * *

Despite the controversial nature of these findings, it must be emphasized that the information is not intended in any way to be an indictment against the Jewish people themselves—hence the differentiation between the designation Jew and Yahwehist.[10] Indeed, there are millions of Yahwehists in the world who are not of Jewish descent; just as there are millions of Jews who are not Yahwehists. Like other forms of bigotry, anti-Semitism is a form of mental and spiritual iniquity, and is not

---

10 The term Yahwehist will be used in this work to denote any follower of the deity Yahweh/Jehovah. This term should not be conflated with the term "Jahwist," which is used by scholars to denote the biblical author who is referred to as J source.

condoned in any way.

Furthermore, progressive Jewish movements are serving to reform the old misconceptions. Some of these amendments can be found in the tenets of the *Kabbalah*.[11] In the eighteenth century, the honorable Moses Mendelssohn also helped to lead a reformative movement called the *Haskalah*, which sought to enlighten through the faculties of reason, spiritual awareness, and human rights. This humanitarian legacy has been advanced in the present day by other reformative Jewish movements, which are serving to help sincere devotees return to the original (*Ein Sof*) source.

---

11 Kabbalah is an esoteric school of thought that is based on Judaism.

CHAPTER II

THE THEOCRACY OF JEHOVAH AND THE MISSION OF THE SAVIOR

While the sands of time were sweeping over the Middle East and covering up the old civilizations of ancient Mesopotamia around the second and first centuries BCE, this historic period of change was not taking place in the region in and around Jerusalem. Instead, the Yahwehist tradition persisted on. This was partially due to an enduring belief that Yahweh had not given up on his chosen people, and that one day a great servant of the Lord would arise in the land; a "Messiah," who would take over where the great pre-exilic kings and legendary prophets left off, and usher in an era of peace and superiority by establishing an independent theocracy dedicated exclusively to Lord Yahweh.

The word "Messiah" is an English rendering of the Hebrew word *Maschiach*, which means "Anointed." This is a reference to the ceremonial process in which a king or high-priest is anointed with oil during a coronation ceremony.

The following examples are passages that seem to refer to the future arrival of a great Savior. Judeo-Christians claim that these are references to "Jesus":

> He shall stand, and shall shepherd in the strength of
> Yahweh, in the majesty of the name of Yahweh his God:

and they will live, for then he will be great to the ends of the earth.

—Micah 5:4

[. . .] He will proclaim peace to the nations. His rule will extend from sea to sea and from the River to the ends of the earth.

—Zechariah 9:10

But he was pierced for our transgressions. He was crushed for our iniquities. The punishment that brought our peace was on him; and by his wounds we are healed.

—Isaiah 53:5

However, once these references are read in context with the rest of the books in which they appear, their original meaning becomes more clear.

It must first be understood that the definition of the Yahwehist Mashiach and Jesus the Christ are actually different—as any rabbi or legitimate scholar will attest. For example, the Mashiach was supposed to be a mighty leader who would be a direct descendant of King David (Isaiah 11:1);[12] however, whether Jesus was a direct descendant of King David is questionable. This is because the genealogies that are reported in the Gospels of Matthew and Luke trace the Davidic ancestral line to Joseph, not to Mary. Although, according to the gospels themselves, Joseph was not the father of Jesus. Furthermore, in both of those gospels the names listed in the ancestral lines are different, and therefore are unreliable. Judeo-Christian apologists claim that Luke's genealogy pertains to Mary; however, ancient tribal identification passed down through the father's side of the family, not the mothers (e.g., Ruth 4:18-22). Furthermore, according to Luke 2:4 it was Joseph, not Mary, who was from the House of David. Likewise, Luke 3:23 clearly states that the listed genealogy pertains to Joseph, not to Mary.[13]

---

12 Jesse is the father of David.

13 It is also telling that, according to Luke 1:36, Mary was related to Elizabeth, who, according to Luke 1:5, was a descendant of Aaron. However, Aaron was not from David's

The Mashiach was also supposed to return all the descendants of Abraham to their homeland where they would live peacefully under the laws of the Torah and be a beacon of light to the world (Isaiah 11:12). However, Jesus never mentioned returning the Jews to their homeland. This is because they had already returned from exile. Furthermore, Jesus did not strictly adhere to the customary laws of Moses (e.g., Mark 2:23-24, 3:1-6; John 5:8-15), which is one of the reasons why the priests were so offended by him. His teachings were also more favorable to the meek and the uneducated, rather than the powerful and the learned (Matthew 5:5). These qualities do not fit with the original description of the mighty Mashiach. Indeed, there is also nothing in the Old Testament that predicts a Maschiach who does not complete his mission the first time. Therefore, there is no legitimate justification for the concept of a resurrection or a "Second Coming." Moreover, according to the Tanakh the Mashiach will be human, not a demi-god; and he will definitely not be God himself. The Christian concept of "the Trinity," in which God manifests in three separate ways: that is, as the Father, the Son, and the Holy Spirit (Matthew 28:19), is actually a heretical concept according to the tenets of traditional monotheistic Judaism. This is because according to the Old Testament/Tanakh itself, "Yahweh is one" (Deuteronomy 6:4). Indeed, Yahweh made it very clear that no one was equal to him (Exodus 20:3; Deuteronomy 32:39).

Old Testament passages that allegedly refer to the Savior can be divided into three separate classifications: (1) Passages that refer to the Yahwehist Mashiach, as opposed to the Christian Christ. (2) Passages that do not refer to any Savior at all, including the Mashiach. (3) Passages in which Jesus makes the intentional effort to fulfill Old Testament prophecy.

In regard to this specific topic, it must be acknowledged that an entire separate book could be written on this subject alone. For now, only a few popular examples of what are believed to be prophecies that refer to Jesus will be more closely examined. The following passage is another source that many Judeo-Christians also cite as messianic prophecy.

---

tribe of Judah, but rather was from the tribe of Levi (Joshua 21:4; Numbers 17:8).

A voice is heard in Ramah, mourning and great weeping, Rachel weeping for her children and refusing to be comforted, because they are no more.

—Yahweh, Jeremiah 31:15

According to this interpretation, the "weeping" for the children that is reported refers to the "Massacre of the Innocents" by King Herod, who allegedly ordered the death of all male children in Bethlehem so as to prevent himself from losing the throne to a future messianic king (Matthew 2:16-17). However, this purported event is not only not corroborated by non-biblical records, such as those of the Jewish historian Flavius Josephus, but it does not even appear in the other gospels. It is also suspicious that this account only appears in the Gospel of Matthew, since, as will be made clear further ahead, the Gospel of Matthew is especially problematic and cannot be considered to be the most accurate of the accounts. It is more likely that the story was inspired by Herod's killing of his own sons—which was an event that actually *was* recorded by Josephus.[14] This was done to prevent his heirs from taking the throne from him. What the author of the Gospel of Matthew did was draw upon this incident in order to suit his own narrative.[2] Furthermore, Ramah was a city that was near Jerusalem. When Jerusalem was conquered by the Babylonians, the captives were taken to Ramah before they were lead away to Babylon (Jeremiah 40:1). Rachel was one of Jacob's wives and was therefore a prominent matriarchal figure. In the passage, the author references Rachel because he believes that she would have mourned the destruction of the Temple and her descendants who had been exiled to Babylon. The weeping for her children is a reference to Genesis 30, where it is written that Rachel was tormented by the fact that she did not have children—which does not have anything to do with Jesus.

Another clear example can be found in the book of Hosea. According to Matthew 2:14-15, Jesus was taken to Egypt for a short time. Many Judeo-Christians claim that this fulfills the prophecy that is found in the book of Hosea; however, this passage in the book of Hosea was never

---

14 The Antiquities of the Jews (Book XVI, XVII)

intended to be prophecy. In this instance, the author speaks for Yahweh:

> When Israel was a child, I loved him, and out of Egypt I called my son. But the more they were called, the more they went away from me. They sacrificed to the Baals and they burned incense to images.
> —Yahweh, Hosea 11.1-2

It is not the Savior who is compared to a "child" and a "son," but rather the people of Israel, which is a common poetic analogue that can be found throughout the Old Testament/Tanakh.[3] We find similar descriptions in Isaiah 41:8-9, as well as the rest of the "servant literature" in the book of Isaiah. This includes Isaiah 53, in which the entire nation of Israel is described as a singular "servant." Therefore, the son coming out of Egypt is actually a reference to the Exodus—which also has nothing to do with Jesus.

It is also peculiar that some Judeo-Christians cite passages in the book of Psalms, which is not even in the "prophetic books." This book is actually considered "wisdom literature," and the writings appearing within were not intended to be prophecy.

Besides all of these cases of forced conflations, it does also appear that Jesus himself also sought to fulfill Old Testament conceptions by making the intentional effort to do so. An example of this is when he did not enter Jerusalem until he was able to do so while riding on a donkey. This was supposedly done so that the king prophecy that is found in Zecharia 9:9 could be fulfilled. In this specific case, Jesus and his followers apparently did endeavor to link themselves with Old Testament scripture that could be interpreted to be prophetic, which was an overt means in which to legitimize their position.

However, what will become apparent moving forward is that even though Jesus was not the Yahwehist Mashiach this does not mean that he was not the Savior. This is because he had his own plan for the salvation of the people.

* * *

According to the traditional Judeo-Christian interpretation, the Christ (i.e., *Christos,* from the ancient Greek word for anointed) submitted himself as a kind of sacrificial scapegoat. By dying for the sins of the people, he was providing some type of way for those who followed his teachings to go to heaven. This is certainly a curious situation that deserves closer examination.

Although he later became known to the world by the Greek translation "Jesus," his original Hebrew name was Yeshua. The gospels report that the priests of Yahweh (i.e., the Pharisees and the Sadducees) believed that Yeshua was a blasphemer. If Yeshua had come to restore the theocracy of Yahweh, why then was he condemned as a heretic? Were the priests simply seeking to fulfill prophecy by violently persecuting the Messiah? One of the reasons why this explanation can be disregarded is because the original Maschiach was never supposed to be persecuted—especially by his own people.

In John 11:49-52, it is reported that the high-priest Caiaphas announced that it would be better for Jesus to die than to risk inciting the Romans against them all. The author of the Gospel of John interprets this as a prophecy; although this was not actually a prophecy in a supernatural sense, but rather a statement that was based on the concerns of the priests.

According to John 5:18, the traditionalists wanted to kill Jesus because not only did he do things such as not strictly adhere to the Mosaic laws but because he dared to make himself equal with God.

Yeshua himself admitted that it was not his initial intention to bring peace, but rather to challenge the status quo:

> I have come to bring fire on the earth, and how I wish it were already kindled! [. . .] Do you think I came to bring peace on earth? No, I tell you, but division.
> —Yeshua, Luke 12:49-51

In the following passage, Yeshua contradicts an Old Testament law that was ordained by Lord Yahweh himself, who told the people that they were to avenge any misdeed that was committed upon them with equal measure; namely, with an "eye for eye, and tooth for tooth" (Exodus 21:23-25):

> You have heard that it was said, 'Eye for eye, and tooth for tooth.' But I tell you, do not resist an evil person. If anyone slaps you on the right cheek, turn to them the other cheek also.
> —Yeshua, Matthew 5:38-39

Yeshua challenged the traditionalists by advocating for a more compassionate type of mentality:

> You have heard it said, 'Love your neighbor and hate your enemy.' But I tell you: Love your enemies and pray for those who persecute you.
> —Yeshua, Matthew 5:43-44

Yahweh made it very clear that anyone who did not obey his laws was to be put to death. One of the methods by which this sentence was to be carried out was by stoning (Numbers 15:35; Ezekiel 23:47). However, in the New Testament Gospel of John (John 8:1-11) we find the well-known account of the woman who was caught committing adultery, which was a stoning offense. According to this account (i.e., the *Pericope Adulterae*),[15] Yeshua interceded and saved her from execution. Instead of the Old Testament "fire and brimstone" mentality, Yeshua advocated for something much different. In his teachings, we do not find the same violence, revenge, hatred, jealousy, and anger that is found in the Old Testament.

> Blessed are the pure in heart, for they shall see God.
> —Yeshua, Matthew 5:8

---

15 The Pericope Adulterae does not appear in the earliest Greek editions of the Gospel of John.[4] I have included this example because I believe, just like the interpolator himself, that it is an example of the type of ethics that Yeshua promoted.

Of course, this way of thinking actually contradicted the actions of Yahweh, who proclaimed the heart to be "deceitful" and "desperately sick" (Jeremiah 17:9).

According to the Old Testament, Yahweh was interested in not only power and fame but in wealth as well (Isaiah 45:3; Haggai 2:8). Yeshua was actually opposed to this type of obsessive materialism:

> How hard it is for rich people to enter the kingdom of God! Indeed, it is easier for a camel to go through the eye of a needle than for a rich person to enter the kingdom of God.
> —Yeshua, Luke 18:24-25

No wonder why the followers of Yahweh considered him to be a heretic. It would seem that Yeshua's teachings contradicted the nature of God. However, what is also perplexing about this situation is that at the same time it appears that Yeshua was also praising the Lord God as well.

Yeshua claimed to have a very personal relationship with God, who he referred to as "the Father":

> Just as the living Father sent me and I live because of the Father, so the one who feeds on me will live because of me. This is the bread that came down from heaven. Your ancestors ate manna and died, but whoever feeds on this bread will live forever.
> —Yeshua, John 6:57-58

The "living Father" gives the "bread" of life to the Son, which is *not* the poisonous bread of the "forefathers." However, the bread (i.e., "manna") that came down from heaven was originally given to the people by Yahweh himself (Exodus 16:4-35). This is a very significant passage. In it, Yeshua indicates that there is a difference between the Father and the deity of the Old Testament.

This next passage may be the most significant of all:

If God were your Father, you would love me, for I have come here from God. I have not come on my own; God sent me. Why is my language not clear to you? Because you are unable to hear what I say. You belong to your father, the devil, and you want to carry out your father's desires. He was a murderer from the beginning, not holding to the truth, for there is no truth in him. When he lies, he speaks his native language, for he is a liar and the father of lies.
—Yeshua, John 8:42-44

Up until this point, the true meaning of this statement has not been understood. In it we are told that "the devil" was the "murderer" who deceived the people into thinking that he was the heavenly Father, when in fact he was the "father of lies."

The traditionalists who were persecuting Yeshua were only seeking to uphold the laws of their Lord; however, Yeshua denounced the "father" of their world as "the devil." Likewise, in Matthew 16:12 Yeshua warns his followers to be on guard against the teachings of the priests of Yahweh. This is because the Pharisees and Sadducees were the preservers of the teachings of the malevolent Lord of Armies. Yeshua called these priests "blind guides," "hypocrites," and the "sons of hell."

A closer look at the gospels themselves reveal that Yahweh was not the heavenly Father of Yeshua. A closer look reveals that the secret mission of Yeshua was actually to *rescue* the people from the wicked Lord of war who disguised himself as the heavenly Father!

This is the reason why Yeshua never referred to his Father by the name Yahweh (i.e., Jehovah). In fact, the name of the Lord of the Old Testament does not even appear in the original New Testament gospels at all!

* * *

Yeshua used parables that alluded to a greater meaning in order to help open the minds of the people and help them to perceive their world in a

40

more clear and unbiased way. This higher meaning is related to what he referred to as "the sacred secrets."

> The knowledge of the secrets of the kingdom of heaven has been given to you, but not to them [. . .] This is why I speak in parables: Though seeing, they do not see; though hearing, they do not hear or understand. In them is fulfilled the prophecy of Isaiah: You will be ever hearing but never understanding; you will be ever seeing but never perceiving. For this people's heart has become calloused; they hardly hear with their ears, and they have closed their eyes. Otherwise they might see with their eyes, hear with their ears, understand with their hearts and turn, and I would heal them.
> —Yeshua, Matthew 13:11-15

Yeshua offered a clue to the nature of the secrets of the kingdom when he revealed that it was not his intention to put new wine (i.e., the new covenant of the heavenly Father) into an old wine-skin (i.e., the old covenant of Yahweh), but rather new wine into a new wine-skin (Mark 2:21).

He also admonished the hardened traditionalists for being bound to the ruler of their world. Of course, the Old Testament itself reports that the ruler of their world was Yahweh (Psalm 47:7).

Just before Yeshua is about to be taken to the Roman authorities, he makes a very important statement to his disciples regarding this ruler:

> I will not say much more to you, for the prince of this world is coming. He has no hold over me.
> —Yeshua, John 14:30

The "prince of this world" was the prince of darkness who resided in a deep "gloom" (Psalm 97:1-2; 1 Kings 8:12; 2 Samuel 22:12; etc.). At that particular time, it was his zealous servants, the Pharisees, who were coming to take him away to the horrific ordeal that they had in store for him.

Most of the people were actually devout traditionalists who were fighting to preserve the institution that their forefathers had allegedly established under the orders of Lord Yahweh himself. As far as the pious and God-fearing people were concerned, evil and sin was disobedience itself; however, Yeshua did not share this belief. In the Gospel of Mark, he defines sin as "greed, malice, deceit," "envy, slander, arrogance," "murder," etc. Of course, these were the qualities of Yahweh himself; hence the following statement:

> All who have come before me were thieves and robbers
> [. . .]
> —Yeshua, John 10:8

Likewise, in the following passage Yeshua declares his intention to "save" the sons of Abraham—that is, to save the sons of Abraham from the God of Abraham:

> Today salvation has come to this house, because this man,
> too, is a son of Abraham. For the Son of Man came to seek
> and to save the lost.
> —Yeshua, Luke 19:9-10

After Yeshua disclosed that the importance of his mission exceeded that of Abraham's (John 8:39-59), the followers of Yahweh immediately took up stones to kill him. We see in these instances that the people had not fallen away from the laws of Yahweh, as is traditionally thought, but rather were resisting Yeshua in order to preserve them! Indeed, Yeshua referred to the old covenant laws, that were supposedly given to Moses by Yahweh himself, as something that was separate from himself and his heavenly Father. This is why he referred to Yahweh's commandments as "their law," and "your law," instead of the will of the Father (John 10:34, 15:25).

* * *

Yeshua made a distinction between his "Father" who is in heaven, as opposed to the chthonic Lord of the "earth":

> The one who comes from above is above all; the one who is from the earth belongs to the earth, and speaks as one from the earth. The one who comes from heaven is above all. He testifies to what he has seen and heard, but no one accepts his testimony.
> —Yeshua, John 3:31-32

In the following passages, Yeshua indicates that the Father is not who they think that it is:

> All things have been delivered to me by my Father. No one knows the Son, except the Father; neither does anyone know the Father, except the Son, and he to whom the Son desires to reveal to him.
> —Yeshua, Matthew 11:27

> No one has seen the Father except the one who is from God; only he has seen the Father.
> —Yeshua, John 6:46

Who then was the Father?

Yeshua was careful not to divulge too much information. Instead, he wisely chose a more subtle approach. This is because if he had stated anything that was overtly anti-Yahweh he would have been rejected and crucified even sooner than he was.

It seems that the Father existed in a higher spiritual state where Yeshua was able to interact with him during events of mystical epiphany. Indeed, in the following passage Yeshua refers to his Father not as a physical being, but rather as a spirit. (Note: The word "God" in the New Testament is translated from the Greek word *Theos*):

God is a spirit. Those who worship him must worship in
spirit and truth.
—Yeshua, John 4:24

According to Yeshua, only he knew who the Father was. This may have
been because he did not believe that the people would be able to
comprehend and accept the controversial and astounding truth. Even the
gnostic Christians, who claimed to know the esoteric teachings of the
Savior, described the Father as "unrevealable."

* * *

The fact that this misunderstanding has been so successfully ingrained
into the popular collective interpretation is certainly a testimony to the
power of the web of misconception and influence that Yahweh and his
agents were so successful in constructing. Yeshua alluded to the nature of
the affected mind in the following passage:

For this reason they could not believe, because, as Isaiah
says elsewhere: "He has blinded their eyes and hardened
their hearts, so they can neither see with their eyes, nor
understand with their hearts, nor turn—and I would heal
them."
—Yeshua, John 12:39-40

Of course, the "he" who is being referred to in this pericope was the Lord
God of Isaiah.
Unfortunately, many people, including many scholars and clergy, are
not only influenced, either consciously or subconsciously, by the
prevailing traditional perspective but many will feel the need to be
respectful of such a sacred belief system—and thus, in some cases,
preserve the security of their careers by offering interpretations that
conform with traditional precepts. This was especially true in previous
centuries. Indeed, those who disagreed with the established interpretation
in previous centuries were also forced to face the consequence of the

death penalty.

Of course, findings that could be perceived as being "anti-Semitic" is an issue as well. However, I contend that the Jewish people should not be defined by the Yahwehists.

One of the reasons why the truth of this situation has not been more clear is because of its complicated nature. In the following verse, for instance, Yeshua seems to refer to the God of Abraham in the same terms as his heavenly Father. Here is how the verse in question reads:

> But concerning the resurrection of the dead, haven't you read that which was spoken to you by God, saying, 'I am the God of Abraham, and the God of Isaac, and the God of Jacob?' God is not the God of the dead, but of the living.
>
> —Yeshua, Matthew 22:31-32

However, in this passage Yeshua does not indicate that Yahweh himself was the God of life, but rather that "God" was a deity who presided over not a dead people, but rather a "living" people; a people who had the ability to be resurrected in the eternal world of spirit. This passage is actually a spiritual and humanistic affirmation, rather than a tribute to Yahweh. The context of this statement (which also appears in Mark 12:26-27 and Luke 20:36-38) is that it occurred at a time when Yeshua was expressing an optimistic belief to the priests of Yahweh that the people would one day be resurrected in heaven where "they can no longer die."

It is true that Yeshua did occasionally refer to the old covenant; however, he did so only as a means of inserting his own point on top of it (e.g., Mark 7.6-8). The situation can be confusing for anyone who is not able to take the context of some of these statements into account. In some accounts, when Yeshua seems to be referring directly to Yahweh, he was actually only making a reference to the historical past. There was always a higher purpose involved when Yeshua invoked the names and the concepts related to the deity of the Old Testament. He guardedly approached the people as a fellow son of Abraham; while at the same time urging them "to get the meaning" of that which was "hidden" from their eyes:

> If you, even you, had only known on this day what would bring you peace—but now it is hidden from your eyes.
> —Yeshua, Luke 19:42

> The kingdom of heaven is like a treasure hidden in the field [. . .]
> —Yeshua, Matthew 13:44

In Luke 6:35, Yeshua refers to his Father as "the Most High" (i.e., *Hypsistos*), which is a reference to the term that appears as *Elyon* in the Hebrew Bible. This is significant since this was one of the epithets that was ascribed to Yahweh. Therefore, this would seem to indicate that Yahweh and the Father were the same; however, the epithet Elyon is actually only a generic title and does not have to specifically refer to Yahweh. Indeed, this epithet did not originally apply to Yahweh, but rather to the Ugaritic/Canaanite god, El.[16]

In John 2:13-16, Yeshua chases out the merchants from the Temple area. In this case, the question must be asked: Why did Yeshua refer to the Temple of Yahweh as his "Father's house"? According to the same book (John 2:17), the reason this was done was in order to fulfill "the words of scripture." This is a reference to Psalm 69:9, in which it is written, "It is the zeal for your house that has consumed me." However, as was previously noted, the book of Psalms was never intended to be prophecy. A more likely reason that Yeshua may have done this was to make a statement about the corrupting link between money and religion. Therefore, Jesus could have been indicating that the Temple should have been a holy shrine dedicated exclusively to *his* heavenly Father, not to Yahweh and his materialistic associates. It is also possible that Yeshua may have never referred to the temple as his Father's house, and that this was an assumption that was made by the scribes who were recording

---

16 The complex difference between El and Yahweh is explained in the Esoteric Edition.

46

events decades later. Indeed, it is now known that the gospels did not begin to be committed down to paper until forty to seventy years after the events occurred, and therefore absolute accuracy should not be expected. Furthermore, as will be made more clear in parts to come, many discrepancies and misleading additions can be found in the gospels.

The other time that this allegedly occurred—and I stress the word *allegedly*—is in Luke 2:46-49, where it is reported that as an adolescent Yeshua referred to the Temple as his "Father's house." However, not only was Yeshua just a child at that time, and therefore was most likely unaware of the true identity of his heavenly Father, but since no scribe was actually present during his childhood, this account cannot be regarded as certain by any means.

* * *

In regard to the concept of the "Trinity," we are left with the question pertaining to the identity of the "Holy Spirit"; or, as it is sometimes referred to as, the "Holy Ghost."

The traditional Judeo-Christian interpretation asserts that the Holy Spirit is a manifestation of God, who is thought to be coincident with both the "Father" (God) and the "Son" (Christ) (Matthew 28:19), and is thought of as a person. However, in these instances the Holy Spirit (*Ruach Kodesh*) is not specifically described as a person, but rather as divine energy, which is the breath of life (i.e., *pneuma*).

> Do not cast me from your presence, or take your Holy
> Spirit from me.
> —Psalm 51:11

When the word is directly associated with Yahweh, it then means "the spirit of God."

Furthermore, referring to the Holy Spirit as a singular "person" violates the precepts of traditional monotheistic Judaism. Indeed, we are explicitly told that "Yahweh is one" (Deuteronomy 6.4), not three. Judeo-Christian apologists will counter that this is not a contradiction because these three forms are manifestations of the same entity (i.e., *homoousios*) —which they relate to the divine essence of God (i.e., *ousia*). However, this interpretation contradicts the original biblical report, which specifically states that it is Yahweh himself who is one.

Judeo-Christians cite passages in the New Testament (e.g., Acts 13:2), in which the Holy Spirit supposedly speaks, in order to justify the personhood of the Holy Spirit; however, these examples are drawn from Pauline sect misunderstandings that occurred at a later time, and therefore are incorrect. (The subject of Pauline misunderstandings will be examined further ahead.)

* * *

In order to understand what is really happening in the gospels, it is necessary to understand the history and authorship of these primary books of the New Testament. Concerning these matters, biblical scholars posit a "two-source hypothesis."[5] The first source has been traced to the Gospel of Mark. However, it is now known that the author of this book was not only not a direct disciple but he was not even Mark the Evangelist, the companion of Peter.[6] Scholars now know that the author of this gospel was actually an anonymous Judeo-Christian scribe, who compiled the accounts from word-of-mouth sources approximately forty years after the events occurred.[7]

Besides the Gospel of Mark, the other original source material that scholars believe that the New Testament authors, such as Matthew and Luke, referred to is the so-called "Q" material (from the German word *Quelle*, meaning "source"). Although the original Q source has yet to be found, most biblical scholars agree that it must have existed.[8]

In the Gospel of Matthew, there is a passage that is neither in the Gospel of Mark nor in the Q source, which contradicts the true mission of the Savior—as well as other passages in the gospels themselves. This is because this statement that was attributed to Yeshua was added at a later time by someone who did not know the secrets of the Savior.

Do not think that I have come to abolish the Law or the Prophets; I have not come to abolish them but to fulfill them. For truly I tell you, until heaven and earth disappear, not the smallest letter, not the least stroke of a pen, will by any means disappear from the Law until everything is accomplished.

—Yeshua, Matthew 5:17-18

Indeed, the Gospel of Matthew is filled with errors. For example, Matthew 27:9 references a passage that is attributed to the prophet Jeremiah together with Judas and thirty pieces of silver, which is presented in a prophetic context; however, no such passage exists in the book of Jeremiah. What is even more telling are the passages in the Gospel of Matthew that contradict information that is reported in the other gospels. For example, in John 21:16 Yeshua refers to Simon Peter as the "son of John," but in Matthew 16:17 he refers to him as the "son of Jonah." In Luke 3:23 it is reported that Joseph was the son of Heli, who was the son of Matthat, the son of Levi, etc., but in Matthew 1:15 it is reported that Joseph was the son of Jacob, who was the son of Matthan, the son of Eleazar, etc. In Luke 11:1-4, it is reported that Yeshua delivered the Lord's Prayer only to the disciples, but in Matthew 6:9-13 (beginning in Matthew 5) he is said to have delivered the Sermon on the Mount before the multitudes. In Luke 23:39, it is reported that only *one* of the criminals who was crucified next to Yeshua insulted him, while the other one accepted Yeshua as the Savior, but in Matthew 27:44 *both* of the criminals "reviled him." In Mark 10:19, Yeshua instructs the people to "honor your father and mother," but in Matthew 10:35 Yeshua causes "division" between a "man and his father, and a daughter against his mother." The Gospel of Matthew not only contradicts information that is recorded in the other gospels but there are even passages in the Gospel of Matthew that contradicts itself! For example, Matthew 1:17 lists fourteen generations between Abraham and David, while Matthew 1:2 lists thirteen. Likewise, Matthew 10:5 and 15:24 report that the gospel was only to be reported to "the lost sheep of Israel," but in Matthew 12:17-21 and 28:19 the gospel was to be spread to the gentiles. In Matthew 5:22,

Yeshua says do not call someone a fool, but in Matthew 23:17 he calls the Pharisees "fools!" This is because the account that is recorded in the Gospel of Matthew is the least accurate of all the gospels.

Although it cannot be denied that some truth may be able to be found in the Gospel of Matthew, using a single passage from this document to argue a point that is out of line with the message that is found repeatedly elsewhere throughout the gospels, including more authentic source material, cannot be justified.[17]

New Testament scholar Bart D. Ehrman presents a strong case in his books: *Misquoting Jesus, Jesus Interrupted, Forged,* and others, that disproves the claim that the Bible is the "inerrant" word of God. His works reveal that no original copies of the Bible exist, and that the copies that do exist are not only from centuries later but contain differences that were both unintentional mistakes as well as intentional edits and additions that were committed by scribes. Furthermore, in a statement that can be applied to Matthew 5:17-18, Ehrman explains:

> In my experience, theologians do not hold to a doctrine because it is found in just one verse; you can take away just about any verse and still find just about any Christian doctrine somewhere else if you look hard enough.
>
> —Bart D. Ehrman, *Jesus Interrupted*

What must be taken into account is that these were documents that were both written and interpreted by man; and even a devout traditionalist cannot honestly deny that man is an imperfect being. Therefore, the previously cited passage, in which Yeshua is reported to have claimed that he did not come to abolish the laws of Yahweh, cannot be considered to be an accurate representation of what he actually said.

Although the author of the Gospel of Matthew is attributed to the disciple of the same name, scholars know that it was actually written by

---

17 This same reasoning can be applied to the controversial passage that is found in Luke 19:27; in which the author (L Source), who was not one of the original disciples, inserted a reference to Jesus demanding that his enemies be brought before him and killed. This is a significant contradiction and is most likely not an accurate representation of what was actually said.

an anonymous scribe, and that the name of the disciple was added as a title to the document at a later time.[9] This was done in order to increase its credibility—which was a common practice during that era.[10] It is evident that the author used the Gospel of Mark, as well as the original Q source, as a reference, which he then infused with the interpretation that was popular among the group of Christians (i.e., the Mattheans) that he was a member of.[11] Scholars believe this group was most likely located in Antioch[12] (modern-day Turkey). Indeed, according to Paul's Epistle to the Galatians (Galatians 2:11-14), Antioch was the location of a Jewish-Christian community who believed in the retainment of Mosaic law (i.e., the "circumcision group"). It was also a group that was specifically affiliated with Peter (i.e., Cephas/Kefa), which explains why Peter is referred to as the "rock" of the Christian movement in, and only in, the Gospel of Matthew (Matthew 16:18). It can therefore be concluded that it was a member of this community (i.e., M source) who inserted favorable references to both Peter and Old Testament law in the Gospel of Matthew.

In this case, some might argue that the community in Antioch could have received direct information from Peter; however, even though Peter was one of the original disciples he cannot be considered to be a reliable source. This is because, according to the gospels themselves—including even the Gospel of Matthew—Peter never understood the secret true mission of the Savior. (This subject will be examined more closely further ahead.)

In summary, it is now known that the gospels were subjected to not only unintentional mistakes but also intentional revisions and editing. Scholars discovered this by comparing earlier versions of the gospels against later ones.[13] In this case, what we find when we delve deeper into the history of the Bible, is a record of inconsistency, mistakes, and even outright deliberate misrepresentation. Therefore, the only way to truly discern what actually took place all those centuries ago is to perceive the underlying essence of the reports, and not allow ourselves to get misled by dubious additions.

* * *

Yeshua understood that his activities would eventually lead to his execution. This heroic act of self-sacrifice reveals the extent of the compassion that he had for a people who were being misled and oppressed by a malevolent trickster and his collaborators, the Pharisees and the Sadducees. Yeshua urged the people to look beyond the repressive "lie," and to "dance" to the music that he was playing (Matthew 11:17). But the roots of incontestable ideology were too firmly planted into the mentality of the people.

At some point, when the time was right, it was his intention to disclose the hidden truth to all those who were ready to hear it. What Yeshua was hoping for was a non-violent revolution that would serve to overturn the laws and the institution of Yahweh gradually; which is why he referred to this revolution in his parables as a seed that would eventually spread and blossom.

There are accounts in the gospels where Yeshua indicates that it was his plan to "ransom" his life for the salvation of many, which would seem to confirm the traditional Judeo-Christian concept of a Messiah who had come to die for the sins of the people. As a result of this interpretation, it is believed by a great majority of Judeo-Christians that all one has to do in order to be saved from damnation is to announce "Jesus Christ as your Lord and Savior" and conform to the Judeo-Christian program. Such misunderstandings propagated a dogmatic and erroneous creed that unscrupulous individuals within the Judeo-Christian institution were even able to use for their own advantage. By instilling the laity with feelings of guilt and shame for their so-called "original sin," as well as constantly reminding them of the painful sacrifice that was made by the Christ for the benefit of humanity, church officials were better able to acquire a significant amount of power and wealth by making the people feel indebted to themselves as the Christ's representatives on Earth.

The truth is that Yeshua did not die *for* the sins of the people, but rather he died *because* of the sins of the people who were misled by the agents of Yahweh. He was willing to undergo this trauma because he believed that his works and his high-profile sacrifice would eventually draw people to his message, and because he knew that both he and everyone else who followed his teachings would be resurrected in heaven.

* * *

After Yeshua's departure, various Christian groups arose. One of the original groups were what is now referred to as the gnostics.

The word gnostic is derived from the Greek word for knowledge (*gnostikos*). It was originally a word that was used to describe intellectuals; although, as far as the original gnostics were concerned, they were simply philosophical (i.e., Neo-Platonist) Christians. However, this term could also be used to indicate that the gnostics were the Christians who *knew* the secret teachings of the Savior.

According to the gnostic-inspired apocryphal Gospel of Mary, Mary (Magdalene)[18] was someone who understood the secret teachings of the Savior and was actively involved in the ministry by helping to teach the true message. However, Peter disapproved of Mary's influence, which seems to be at least partially due to his traditional views regarding the role of women. Indeed, the schism that occurred between Mary and Peter is recorded in other texts as well.[19]

Of course, the other branch of Christianity that arose during that formative time was Peter and Paul's sect. In the early years, the different Christian groups competed against each other. The rivalry even extended to a personal level between Peter and the gnostic-influenced Simon Magus.[20] In the apocryphal book the Acts of Peter, Simon and Peter are recorded directly competing with one another. Of course in this version, which is presented by the followers of the Petrine/Pauline (i.e., Peter and Paul) sect, Simon is depicted as a foolish charlatan, and Peter as a righteous victor. (Although the apostle Peter played a role in what has become so-called "orthodox" Christianity, no single person was as influential as Paul. Therefore, Peter and Paul's sect will henceforth be referred to as the "Paulines.") In this account, it is reported that Simon

---

18 There has been some debate regarding which Mary this refers to; however, the gnostics knew that it was Mary Magdalene who was the special beloved one of the Savior.

19 The Gospel of Thomas; the Pistis Sophia; the (Greek) Gospel of the Egyptians.

20 Simon Magus is actually considered more of a proto or quasi gnostic.

had the ability to levitate high up into the air, and while he was displaying that ability to the people Peter prayed for him to fall to the ground. After Peter's prayers were answered and Simon plummeted to the ground, the crowd proceeded to stone him to death.

In another story that is recorded in the Pauline New Testament (Acts 8:9), Simon is said to have even resorted to the nefarious scheme of attempting to bribe Peter and John into giving him the ability to cure by the laying on of hands—a practice that has come to be known as "Simony." Simon was also given the title "Magus," which would seem to indicate that he was a practitioner of magic; however, the three heralded wise-men who visited the infant Savior in Bethlehem were also said to be magi. (That is, if we were to assume that the account that is reported in Gospel of Matthew is accurate.)

According to the second-century Pauline bishop Irenaeus,[21] among some of the other so-called "heresies" that were committed by Simon the Magus and his gnostic followers (i.e., the Simonians) was their practice of the "magical arts." These practices allegedly included the reciting of incantations—which may have actually been nothing more than liturgical hymns and prayers—as well as the making of love potions, the exorcism of spirits, and the communication with spirits. However, most of these accusations could have been leveled at Yeshua the Savior as well.

Another one of the alleged heresies of Simon Magus was his teaching that the Old Testament god was not the highest God.[22] Of course, such a proclamation was not well-received by the Paulines; and as a result, Simon was unjustly vilified.

Another unconventional notion that offended the Judeo-Christian[23] "orthodox," pertained to the gnostic belief that there were other divine beings besides Yeshua—such as Derdekeas, Hermes Trismigestus, and Mirotheos (i.e., Meirothea). However, Yeshua himself is recorded instructing his disciples, in even the canonical gospels, to go forth and do as he did; which meant that they themselves were to help save their world

---

21 Against Heresies (Book I)

22 Clementine Homilies III (Chapter 10)

23 The term "Judeo-Christian" will be used (as opposed to Christian) as a way in which to designate the Christians (e.g., Paulines) who accept Yahweh and the scriptures of the Old Testament.

by becoming saviors according to their own abilities. This concept is exemplified in the walking on water story, for instance, in which Yeshua invited the disciples to perform miracles along with him. Of course, to the priests of "Jehovah"—which is the anglicized Latin name for Yahweh—such supernatural ability was considered to be sorcery.

Yeshua urged the people to discover and develop the latent divinity that was within themselves, and to teach and heal others just as he himself had done. Inspired individuals, such as Simon Magus and the gnostic Persian prophet Mani, were only seeking to fulfill this very teaching.

* * *

The second- and third-century AD Judeo-Christian author Tertullian, directed his condemnation against a Christian man named Marcion. According to Tertullian,[24] Marcion was a devious barbarian from Sinope in Pontus, where residents supposedly engaged in cannibalism and freely partook of "libidinous desires" without shame. Marcion's other purported crime was that he preached the existence of "two gods"—which pertained to the difference between Yahweh and the Father. Although, Marcion did not directly equate Yahweh with the devil, but rather with the "Demiurge." (The subject of the Demiurge will be examined further ahead.)

Despite Tertullian's accusation that Marcion was a barbarian, records[25] indicate that Marcion was actually born into an upper-class Judeo-Christian family (his father was a bishop), and that he himself was a "ship-master." Marcion even highly regarded Paul, and included his writings in his own collection (i.e., the *Apostolikon*). It is also peculiar that Tertullian described Sinope as barbaric, since the city was actually settled by the Greeks. Furthermore, far from being an unrestrained sexual deviant, Marcion preached the value of celibacy.[26] One of the differences

---

24 Five Books Against Marcion (Book I)

25 Five Books Against Marcion (Book I); The Panarion (i.e., Against Heresies) (Book I, part 42) by Epiphanius of Salamis.

26 The Panarion (i.e., Against Heresies) (Book I, part 42) by Epiphanius of Salamis.

between Marcionite and Pauline Christianity, was that Marcion permitted woman to attain important positions in the church.[27] Other than this, it seems that the only significant difference that set him apart from the Paulines was that he knew that the Old Testament god was not the heavenly Father of Jesus. To him this was not secret knowledge, but rather only common sense! It could be said that Marcion even wrote the first version of the book that you are now reading when he compiled the sayings of Jesus and compared them to the sayings of Jehovah, in order to show the contradictions between these two individuals, in his book *Antitheses*.[28]During those early years, the Marcionite branch was so successful that it even rivaled that of the Paulines. In some regions, Marcionism was even the dominant form of Christianity.[14] However, it was Paul's sect that of course reigned supreme when they—among other reasons—received the support of the Roman emperors. It was this consolidation that worked to finally stamp out the competitive influence of the other Christian groups.

It was during that time that the Hebrew name Yeshua was changed to the Greek *Iesous*, and then again to the Latin *Iesus*; which eventually lead to the English rendering, *Jesus*. (Henceforth, Yeshua will be referred to as Jesus—which signifies his revised Judeo-Christian identity.)

* * *

In 1945, an earthenware jar was uncovered by local farmers in Nag Hammadi Egypt. When the jar was broken open, papyrus pages bound together into thirteen leather codices were discovered. The books had clearly been intentionally buried in order to preserve them from Pauline censorship.

Among the writings in the gnostic Nag Hammadi collection that make a reference to the secret teachings of the Savior is the Gospel of Thomas, which is a text that can be dated as far back as the gospels of the New Testament.[15] In this record are further references to "hidden" matters, and

---

27 The Panarion (i.e., Against Heresies) (Book I, part 42) by Epiphanius of Salamis.

28 Antitheses is no longer extant; however, references to it appear in Five Books Against Marcion (Book II) by Tertullian, and Refutation of All Heresies (Book VII) by Hippolytus.

a quote that directly refutes Old Testament law:

> His disciples said to him, "Is circumcision useful or not?"
> He [Jesus] said to them, "If it were useful, their father
> would produce children already circumcised from their
> mother. Rather, the true circumcision in spirit has become
> profitable in every respect."
> —Nag Hammadi Codices, Gospel of Thomas

In the following passage, Jesus indicates that the underlying truth that he
was alluding to would not be easy for the people to accept, since it was
such a controversial and astounding revelation:

> Let him who seeks continue seeking until he finds. When
> he finds, he will become troubled. When he becomes
> troubled, he will be astonished, and he will rule over all.
> —Jesus, Nag Hammadi Codices, The Gospel of Thomas

The next passage is especially significant. Based on Thomas's reaction, it
is evident that Jesus had told him the difference between Yahweh and the
Father:

> And he [Jesus] took him [Thomas], and withdrew, and
> spoke three sayings to him. When Thomas came back to
> his friends they asked him, "What did Jesus say to you?"
> Thomas said to them, "If I tell you one of the sayings he
> spoke to me, you will pick up rocks and stone me, and fire
> will come from the rocks and devour you."
> —Nag Hammadi Codices, The Gospel of Thomas

The gnostic account also emphasized a more humanistic ideology; a
Christianity that was based not on the authority of a hierarchical
institution, but from within every single person:

> If those who lead you say to you, "See, the Kingdom is in

the sky," then the birds of the sky will precede you. If they say to you, "It is in the sea," then the fish will precede you. Rather, the Kingdom is inside of you, and it is outside of you. When you come to know yourselves, then you will become known, you will realize that it is you who are the sons of the living Father. But if you do not know yourselves, you dwell in poverty and it is you who are that poverty.

—Jesus, Nag Hammadi Codices, The Gospel of Thomas

That which you have will save you if you bring it forth from yourselves.

—Jesus, Nag Hammadi Codices, The Gospel of Thomas

Beware that no one lead you astray, saying, "Lo here," or "Lo there!" For the Son of Man is within you.

—Jesus, The Gospel of Mary,

Gnostic teaching, which placed a greater emphasis on spirituality, philosophy, and individuality, presented a subversive threat to the authoritative institution that the Pauline bishops, priests, and deacons were endeavoring to establish.

While Jehovah had condemned the self-empowered individual, according to the gnostics, Jesus had actually praised such a person:

Blessed are the solitary and elect.

—Jesus, Nag Hammadi Codices, The Gospel of Thomas

Of course, such a type of Christianity would not have appealed to the Roman emperors, who required a creed that would bolster their own power by creating a society of workers, warriors, and worshipers; and thus help to preserve their fractured empire. What they needed was not individual wisdom, spirituality, and self-discovery, but rather a system that turned the people's attention toward service to God, King, and Country.

Indeed, Machiavelli was aware of the advantages of the merging of church and state, just as the Roman emperors before him:

> For though they [ecclesiastical principalities] [. . .] may be kept [. . .] because they are sustained by ancient laws rooted in religion that have proved capable of keeping princes in power no matter how they live or rule [. . .] And since they are sustained by superior causes which transcend human understanding, I will not discuss them because they are supported and exalted by God, it would be an act of presumption and rashness to speak of them.
> —Niccolo Machiavelli, *The Prince*

> Sovereignties, in particular possess strength, unity, stability, only to the degree to which they are sanctified by religion.
> —Niccolo Machiavelli, *The Prince*

* * *

Unlike their Pauline counterparts, the gnostics did not band together to form any singular institutional authoritative council. The result was a variety of supernatural characters, arcane cosmologies, and philosophic theologies that were not only not always in complete accord but were also mostly unintelligible to the lay-person. This is, most likely, one of the reasons why the Pauline sect was able to take over the interpretation.

Some of the gnostic Christian groups that arose during that early period were the Valentinians and the Sethians; each of which were named after their founding teachers. Most of the information that was recorded about these groups were documented by their Pauline opponents (e.g., Epiphanius and Irenaeus). The result is a distorted interpretation that accuses some of these groups, such as the so-called "Borborites" (although they were more likely originally known as the Barbeloites) and the Carpocratians, of engaging in bloody and sexual sacraments. However, it is unlikely that these descriptions are accurate. In fact, most gnostics saw the physical world as corrupt, and sought to free themselves from captivity to this world by focusing on matters related to the eternal spirit. Furthermore, according to the gnostic Book of Thomas the Contender, engaging in "polluted intercourse" was something that was discouraged. It is also ironic that the Paulines would make such accusations, since similar charges were leveled at them by the pagans (e.g., the Greek philosopher Celsus).[16]

In the second century of the Common Era, the proto-orthodox bishop Irenaeus of Lyons urged his followers to condemn the gnostics.[29] This hostile polemic set the precedent for the years of strife and persecution that were to follow.

One of the original Christian patriarchs who may have been aware of the secrets of the Savior and who was also accused of heresy was James "the Just." This individual may have not only been one of the original disciples (not to be confused with the apostle James, son of Zebedee) but may have even been Jesus's half-brother as well (Galatians 1:19). Moreover, according to the Gospel of Thomas, Jesus did not name Peter as the future leader of the movement, but rather James the Just.

In the following passage, James admonishes the people for having been deceived by the wrong "Lord":

> The Lord has taken you captive from the Lord, having closed your ears, that they may not hear the sound of my word.
> —James, Nag Hammadi Codices, The Second Apocalypse of James

He then goes on to say that he shall "doom to destruction" the house that they believe that God has made. The Yahwehist crowd reacted to what they perceived as blasphemy by seizing him and burying him halfway into the ground before stoning him to death.

* * *

---

29   Against Heresies (*Adversus Haereses*)

In the following gnostic document, Jesus refers to the Machiavellian "schemes" that were used by the malevolent ruler to assert his selfish will:

> [. . .] his gifts are not blessings. His promises are evil schemes.
> —Jesus, Nag Hammadi Codices, The Second Apocalypse of James

The gnostics knew that Yahweh/Jehovah masqueraded as the heavenly Father. Although they did not refer to him as either Yahweh or Jehovah, but rather as "Yaldabaoth."[30]

> When he [Yaldabaoth] gazed upon his creation surrounding him, he said to his host of demons, the ones who had come forth from out of him: "I am a jealous God and there is no God but me!"
> —Nag Hammadi Codices, The Apocryphon of John

The gnostics also referred to Jehovah as Sakla/Saclas (the fool) and Samael (the blind god/god of the blind).

> But Ialdabaoth, Saclas, who possesses many forms in order to reveal himself with diverse forms as he pleases [. . .]
> —Nag Hammadi Codices, The Apocryphon of John

---

30 The most prominent etymological interpretation of the name Yaldabaoth (i.e., Yaltabaoth, or Ialdabaoth) is that it could mean "child of chaos" (*yalda bahut*);[17] although this interpretation is contested by some scholars. Gershom Scholem (a prominent twentieth-century scholar of Jewish mysticism) postulated that the name is most likely a composite of the words *Yald* and *Sabaoth*.[18] The Hebrew root YLD could indeed mean child; however, it could also be a reference to the verb form, which means "to beget." This not only relates to the Aramaic use of the term but also relates to his description as the "begetter" in the gnostic texts (e.g., the Sophia of Jesus Christ). Furthermore, if *abaoth* derives from the Hebrew word *sabaoth*, this would indicate that Yaldabaoth was the begetter of armies—which is a reference to Yahweh Sabaoth.

Lord Saclas Yaldabaoth[31] was not the heavenly Father, but rather the "Demiurge."

The word Demiurge is derived from the Greek word for public or people worker, which signified his role as the creator, or "craftsmen," of the physical world of mortal beings. Although the philosopher Plato and the Neo-Platonists saw the Demiurge as a supernatural Creator, it was the gnostics who relegated him to the creator of not only the inferior material world but also identified him with the wicked god of the Old Testament.

The Demiurge was able to gain power for himself through the use of fear, violence, and deceptive schemes. The conditioning of mental perspective led to what enlightened sages refer to as the veil of illusion.

> And thus when the world came to be in distraction, it wandered astray throughout time. For all the men who are on earth served the demons from the foundation until the consummation of the Aeon—the angels served justice and the men served injustice. Thus the world came to be in a distraction and an ignorance and a stupor. They all erred until the appearance of the true man.
> —Nag Hammadi Codices, On the Origin of the World

The "true man" was the Savior, who came at the end of the age to help free the servants of the Lord of Armies.

> That which was revealed to me was hidden from everyone and shall only be revealed through him [. . .] I hasten to make them free and want to take them above him who wants to rule over them.
> —Jesus, Nag Hammadi codices, The Second Apocalypse

---

31 According to the Gospel of Judas, Yaldabaoth was also referred to as "Nebro, which means 'rebel'." In this account, Saklas is described as an assistant to Nebro, which differs from the account that is found in the Apocryphon of John. Furthermore, if Nebro is the same individual who is called "Nebruel" in the gnostic Holy Book of the Great Invisible Spirit text (i.e., the Coptic Gospel of the Egyptians), this would be another differing account. It is likely that these discrepancies represent different understandings that were held by different gnostic individuals and groups.

of James

In the following passage, Jesus encourages the people to discern the difference between the one who rules over them and the Father:

> His promises are evil schemes. For you are not an instrument of his compassion, but it is through you that he does violence [. . .] But understand and know the Father who has compassion.
> —Jesus, Nag Hammadi codices, The Second Apocalypse of James

> Hear and understand—for a multitude, when they hear, will be slow witted. But you, understand as I shall be able to tell you. Your father is not my father.
> —Jesus, Nag Hammadi Codices, The Second Apocalypse of James

* * *

The Christians faced significant persecution during the early years. One especially zealous antagonist was a man named Saul. Saul was a Greek Jew who was not only a Pharisee but was also a Roman citizen.

According to the account that is recorded in the book of Acts, Saul was traveling down a road on his way to Damascus to deliver letters to the high-priests that would petition for the rejection of the Christians, when he was blinded by a white light. Inside the light he heard the voice of the Christian Savior who spoke to him asking, "Why are you persecuting me?" After having witnessed the vision, Saul underwent a conversion of faith; and, after changing his name to Paul, he became a devout follower of Jesus.

Although Paul had undergone a profound experience and transformation, he was still prone to the ideology that his upbringing had instilled in him. By linking the Father with Jehovah, he was better able to make that monumental leap of faith. Unfortunately, no single person

63

played as much of an influence in propagating the mistaken interpretation of Christianity to the world than Paul of Tarsus.

While it is true that Paul was a proponent of "love" (1 Corinthians 13), he also urged his followers to "become slaves of God" (Romans 6:22), and "slaves of Christ" (1 Corinthians 7:22). He also warned against provoking "the Lord's jealous anger" (1 Corinthians 10:22), and to beware of "the wrath of God" (Romans 1.18). He also exhorted his followers to cultivate "obedience of faith" (Romans 1:5), so that their "faith might rest not on human wisdom but on the power of God" (1 Corinthians 2:5). Likewise, he emphasized the importance of following without "questioning" (Philippians 2:14), and to work towards salvation with "fear and trembling" (Philippians 2:12). He also instructed the members of his sect to "follow the faith of Abraham" (Romans 4:16), and to "hold fast to traditions" (1 Corinthians 11:2) so as to "confirm the promises of the patriarchs" (Romans 15:8). He also continually cited passages from the Old Testament/Tanakh in order to justify his mistaken reasoning (Romans 9). Paul was a rigidly devout man. He apparently saw himself not as a humanitarian and enlightened benefactor, but rather as a "prisoner of Christ" (Ephesians 3:1)[32] and an "ambassador in chains" (Ephesians 6:20).

> Slaves, obey your earthly masters with respect and fear, and with sincerity of heart, just as you would obey Christ. Obey them not only to win their favor when their eye is on you, but as slaves of Christ, doing the will of God from your heart.
> —Ephesians 6:5

Paul had been conditioned all his life to believe that virtue was to be found in self-sacrifice, suffering, obedience, tradition, and servitude to Lord Yahweh. However, Jesus himself indicated, in even the Pauline New Testament itself, that he thought of his disciples neither as servants nor as slaves, but rather as "friends" (John 15:14). Indeed, other differences can

---

32 Scholars do not believe that the Epistle to the Ephesians was written by Paul. Nevertheless, this book does reflect the Pauline perspective.

64

be found between the teachings of Jesus and Paul. For example, Mark 2:15 records that Jesus ate with sinners, but according to 1 Corinthians 5:11, Paul instructed his followers *not* to eat with sinners. Furthermore, Jesus emphasized the value of repentance (Luke 3:3, 13:3), while Paul emphasized the value of faith (Romans 1:17, 3:26-28). It can also be said that Paul inadvertently contradicted the teachings of Jesus when he put "new wine into old wine-skin"—that is, when he conflated the heavenly Father and his son with Yahweh/Jehovah.

According to Paul's own interpretation, Israel was in need of a Savior because they thought that they could achieve salvation through the works of law rather than by faith (Romans 9:31-32). It was also Paul who helped to emphasis not only servitude to Yahweh/Jehovah but submission to the death of the Christ. Paul also claimed that he received his knowledge through "revelation" (Galatians 1:12); although, according to the account that is recorded in the book of Acts, Jesus did not reveal any special information to him—especially information related to the secret matters.

Paul was generally an ethically-minded man who truly wanted to do the right thing, and did so to the best of his ability; although, he was not present during the time when Jesus was referring to the underlying secret truth of his mission. Indeed, Paul even admits to at times being "perplexed" by the situation (2 Corinthians 4:8).

In the following passage, Paul attempts to explain why the people rejected the Savior by referring to a quote from the Old Testament:

> God gave them a spirit of stupor, eyes that could not see
> and ears that could not hear, to this very day.
> —Paul, Romans 11:8

Unfortunately, Paul did not realize how far the confusion extended. When Jesus was denouncing the Pharisees as "blind guides" (Matthew 15:9-14), these words could have been directed at Paul; a man who had been one of these priests himself.

* * *

Paul was not the only one who misunderstood the true meaning of the mission of Jesus. The other was one of the original disciples himself, Simon Peter.

Roman Catholic Paulines often cite a passage that is found in the Gospel of Matthew (16:18), where Jesus supposedly refers to Peter as the foundational "rock" of the future Christian movement. However, this passage is found only in the Gospel of Matthew, which, as was previously noted, is the least reliable of all the gospels. It is also telling that a similar conversation appears in the gnostic Gospel of Thomas; although, in this version there is no mention of Peter being declared the foundation stone of a future movement. It is evident that this reference was inserted by what scholars refer to as the "M source."

The reason why Jesus *may* have especially regarded Peter was because of the sincerity of his optimistic faith. Indeed, that is the context of the quote, which occurred directly after Peter declared Jesus to be "the Christ, the Son of the living God." Therefore, if this quote is accurate, it could mean that Jesus meant that he would build the church of the Father upon the type of faith in his divinity that was professed by Peter.

It must also be kept in mind that in the very same gospel there are also instances of Jesus actually rebuking Peter for not understanding what he was doing and what was supposed to happen. In Matthew 16:21-24, for instance, Peter protests Jesus's destiny to be harmed by the elders of Jerusalem, which ends with Jesus turning to Peter and saying, "Get behind thee Satan!" Jesus also admonished Peter for not understanding one of his parables (Matthew 15:16), and even asked Peter if he was "dull" (or "without understanding" in other translations). Peter is again admonished when his faith wavered when he attempted to walk on water (Matthew 14:31), and again for falling asleep in Gethsemane (Matthew 26:36-45). When Judas brought the authorities to seize Jesus, it was Peter who took out a sword and cut off the ear of a servant of one of the high-priests (John 18:10-11). During that incident, Jesus reprimanded Peter again for not only acting out in violence but for not understanding what was supposed to take place. This misunderstanding is also reflected in the book of the Acts of the Apostles, in which Peter announces to the crowd that it is the "God of Abraham, the God of Isaac, and the God of Jacob, the God of our ancestors," who has "glorified his servant Jesus" (Acts 3:13).

Although Peter was obviously a devout and well-meaning person, it is evident that he never fully understood the true meaning of the mission of the Savior. This is most likely because Jesus felt that Peter—who was clearly what could be described as a simpleton—would not have been able to handle the astounding truth, and therefore never directly told him.[33] Therefore, if Jesus called Peter the cornerstone rock of the future Christian movement, it was a statement that was clearly based on Peter's optimistic disposition, rather than his mental comprehension.

* * *

In the early fourth century AD, the Romans were fighting among themselves for control of a declining empire. It was during that time that Emperor Constantine allegedly experienced a revelation (most likely in a dream) concerning a Christian symbol. (A monogramatic Christogram in the form of a *labarum*.)[34] Constantine went on to be victorious in battle. As a result, he converted and issued the Edict of Milan, which officially sanctioned the Pauline sect.

Why then was this particular group chosen, as opposed to the others that were also around during that time, such as the Montanists,[35] the Ebionites,[36] the Marcionites, and gnostic groups such as the Manicheans? There are several reasons for this: (1) The Paulines were likely the most

---

33 According to the gnostic Apocryphon of James text, James and Peter were both told the sacred secret. However, the Apocryphon of James is not only a second- to fourth-century AD pseudonymous work but the entire text does not accord well with other gnostic accounts and ideology. The account seems to be the author's—most likely a man known to scholars as Cerinthus—own interpretation of events.[19] Therefore, this contradiction can be dismissed as an isolated aberration.

34 The labarum (i.e., the *chi rho*) is a symbol that is formed from the first two letters of the Greek word for Christ, which appear as the letter P superimposed over the letter X.

35 The Montanists were an early Christian sect that engaged in ecstatic prophecy and emphasized a conservative lifestyle.

36 The Ebionites were an early ascetic Jewish Christian movement who saw Jesus as the Jewish Messiah and rejected Paul and the gentile world.

67

active sect in Rome at that time, and therefore may have been the most familiar to Constantine. (2) The Paulines were organized into a manageable hierarchical regime who were willing to submit themselves to authority systems.

> Remind them to be in subjection to rulers and to authorities, to be obedient, to be ready for every good work.
> —Titus 3:1[37]

(3) The Pauline sect would have also been seen as more legitimate than some of the others because of its connection with a long-standing Old Testament tradition—as opposed to the Marcionites and the gnostics, who rejected the Old Testament. Therefore, the Paulines would have been perceived as more of an authentic religious institution, rather than a mere fledgling cult.[20] (4) The Ebionites required members to strictly observe Yahwehist law, which included not only not eating certain kinds of meat but circumcision as well. It also seems that the Ebionites were devoted to lives of poverty (the name Ebionite itself most likely derives from the Hebrew word *ebyonim*, which can be translated as "the poor ones"). It is likely that such requirements would not have been appealing to the gentiles—especially to Constantine; despite the fact that Jesus himself spoke out against those who hoarded wealth. Moreover, the Ebionites had no intention of integrating with the gentiles. (5) The Roman Pauline orthodox were not as elitist as the gnostics, and therefore were more accessible to the common citizen. Indeed, this is what the word "catholic"[38] refers to.

This turn of events proved to be a crushing setback for other Christian groups, as persecution by the Paulines, who had the enforcement power of the Roman army behind them, increased.

It was also during that formative period that the books of the Bible

---

37 See also Romans 13:1.

38 The word "Catholic" is derived from the Greek word *katholikismos*, which means "all-embracing," "universal," or "according to the whole." It is a word that represents the belief that this Pauline denomination teaches the whole truth and represents all of Christianity.

were being collected and edited, as the records of the Old Testament/Tanakh were combined with the books of the New Testament. It was a mistake that would serve to justify the centuries of human rights abuses that followed.

Due to the misunderstandings of those early Christians, what happened is that the priesthood of Yahweh was essentially carried over to the priesthood of Jehovah. What happened next was the most consequential and ironic twist in all of human history. Instead of a doctrine that was centered on the life and true teachings of the Savior and the compassionate heavenly Father, a dogmatic creed was founded that was based on the death of the Christ and servitude to Lord Jehovah.

> Some who do not understand mystery speak of things that which they do not understand, but they will boast that the mystery of the truth is theirs alone [. . .] But immediately they join with one of those who misled them [. . .] They do business in my word, and they propagate harsh fate.
> —Jesus, Nag Hammadi codices, The Apocalypse of Peter

What the Paulines did was build up a grand Christology that turned a young rabbi healer and reformer from Galilee into "God" himself. However, what should be understood is that the movement that was begun by Yeshua was never originally intended to be its own separate gentile religion, nor was Yeshua God.

Judeo-Christianity was able to succeed not only because of the support that it received from the Roman empire but because it did indeed fulfill basic human needs related to security and community. Nevertheless, it should be understood that it is an institution that is based on the greatest misunderstanding of all time.

* * *

The next step in the great misconception was when the book of Revelation was added to the New Testament. This final book of the Pauline collection is also known as the "Apocalypse of John."

69

The word "apocalypse" is derived from the Greek word *apokalypsis*, which literally translates as "revelation," or "unveiling." The document was written late in the first century (circa 95 AD) by a man who is referred to as "John the Revelator," or "John of Patmos." These epithets are used to distinguish him from John the disciple, who would have been of an improbable age—especially in that era. It is also telling that, according to Acts 4:13, John the disciple was described as "uneducated" (i.e., illiterate). Indeed, scholars who have examined the original text do not believe that the book of Revelation was written by the original disciple of the same name.[21] Even the early Judeo-Christian scholar Dionysius did not believe that this book was written by John the disciple.[22] Indeed, the author of Revelation never even made the direct claim that he was John the disciple.

It is also known that the apocryphal Acts of John, as well as the Acts of Peter, Andrew, and Thomas, were not written by John the disciple, but rather by a man named Leucius Charinus.[23] This practice of titling a text with the name of one of the original disciples was a way to make the work seem more authentic.[39]

> To give authority to the vision, the apocalyptist (the author of the apocalypse) takes on the name of a great figure of the past, an apostle or a patriarch of the Old Testament. To increase its prophetic value, the work is usually placed in the past; thus the prophecy of future history can be proved correct (because in fact these earlier events have already occurred).
>
> —Willis Barnstone, *The Other Bible*

There were other eschatological works (i.e., apocalypses) besides the Revelation of John (e.g., the Apocalypses of Peter, Ezra, and Baruch) that were circulating among the Christians during the early years as well. None of these books were written by the individuals that they were attributed to.

---

39 New Testament scholar Bart D. Ehrman provides further elucidation on this topic in his books, *Forged* (Harper One, 2011).

Common themes among these apocalypses include a resurrected new Jerusalem, a great war, as well as a trial by fire and a final day of judgment. Not only do modern-day scholars believe that these texts are fraudulent but even the original compilers of the Bible as well. Indeed, the book of the Revelation of John was not included in the earliest compilations of the New Testament. The inclusion of Revelation appears to have been mostly due to the efforts of one man alone, the Pauline bishop, Athanasius.[24]

In another text that is referred to as the Apocalypse of Peter (not to be confused with the gnostic text of the same name), Jesus is used in the role of Jehovah, in much the same way that he is represented in the book of Revelation. In this account, Peter is taken up into another world where he is shown the hellish punishments of those who turned away from the Lord's "righteousness." Among other horrors, they are hung by their tongues and hair, and heated iron and "rays of fire" are forced into their eyes. According to the account, Peter is led there by Jesus himself, who tells him that his Father has the power to command the forces of hell.

It is evident that the authors of these pseudo-apocalypses, including the Revelation of John, simply used the Old Testament books of Zechariah, Ezekiel, and Daniel, as models for their own work. In the following passage, for instance, we find the inspiration behind the four horsemen of the Apocalypse that is found the book of Revelation:

> Again I lifted up my eyes, and saw, and behold, four chariots came out from between two mountains; and the mountains were mountains of brass. In the first chariot were red horses; in the second chariot black horses; in the third chariot white horses; and in the fourth chariot dappled horses, all of them powerful.
> —Zechariah 6:1-3

In the Apocalypse of Zechariah, we also find seven "lamp-stands" of the light of the Lord, as well as the same type of "scrolls," "crowns," "prophecies," "Daughter of Babylon," and the hellish punishments that await the disobedient. All of these symbols and afflictions are related to "the curse that is going out over the whole land" that is ordered by Jehovah. Likewise, the leviathan dragon images that appear in the book of Revelation were lifted from Psalm 74:14, Jeremiah 51:34, and Ezekiel 32:2.

In these apocalyptic stories are references to a great Machiavellian war that is to come, in which the Lord will cause everyone to "attack each other." Most of the people will be wiped out with biological weapons in the form of plague.

We are told in the book of Revelation that a man named "John" was approached by a divine being who "was like the Son of man"—that is, someone who was *like* Jesus. Initially, the divine being only identifies himself as the one who "holds the seven stars in his right hand," and the one who holds "the keys of death and hell" (Revelation 1:17-18). We are eventually led to believe that the divine being is Jesus; however, according to the gospels, Jesus himself indicated that he held the keys to the kingdom of the heavenly Father (Matthew 16:19), not to death and hell. It is therefore much more likely that the individual who is described is someone who represents Jehovah.

John is then supposedly told a "sacred secret" that began with the "prophet" "slaves" of the Old Testament. A secret that will be consummated in a new Judeo-Christianized era (Revelation 10:7). He is eventually taken into a throne room, where an elaborate pageant is played out before him. In this symbolic performance, the Savior is represented as a "Lamb." Through the use of sorrow, compassion, remorse, guilt, and fear, the people will feel compelled to surrender their hearts and minds to the institution of the wounded lamb that will rule over the Earth.

In the following passage, the Lord praises those who did not figure out the so-called "deep things of Satan." This may be a reference to the gnostic and/or Marcionite Christians, who were aware of the difference between Yahweh/Jehovah and the heavenly Father.

> But the rest of you in Thyatira—all who don't hold on to
> Jezebel's teaching, who haven't learned what are called the
> deep things of Satan—I won't burden you with anything
> else. Just hold on to what you have until I come. I have

received authority from my Father. I will give authority over the nations to everyone who wins the victory and continues to do what I want until the end. Those people will rule the nations with iron scepters and shatter them like pottery.
—Revelation 2:24-27

Of course, Jesus himself never spoke of ruling over the people with an iron rod and breaking them into pieces.

In the following passage, we find more references to the slavery and fear that Jesus had sought to abolish:

Praise our God, all you his servants, you who fear him, both great and small!
—Revelation 19:5

In Revelation 22:16, the author begins speaking as Jesus himself, saying that it is "I, Jesus" who inspired the Apocalypse. However, this simply is not true. Indeed, Jesus warned that the minions of the devil would attempt to use his name and usurp his identity after his departure:

Be careful not to let anyone deceive you. Many will come using my name. They will, 'I am he,' and they will deceive many people.
—Jesus, Mark 13:5-6

When you see "the abomination that causes desolation" standing where it does not belong—let the reader understand [. . .]
—Jesus, Mark 13:14

The "abomination that causes desolation" is the "Almighty" "Lord of Armies." The place where "he does not belong" is on the throne next to the "Lamb." The truth is that the abomination was the same being that Jesus referred to as the "Father of the lie" (John 8:44).

Jesus knew that the forces of Yahweh would try to thwart him, both during and after his ministry. He tried to prepare the people for this inevitable scheme when he warned them about "false prophets" (Mark 13:21-22). In the following passage, Jesus tells the people how to identify false prophets:

> Watch out for false prophets. They come to you in sheep's clothing, but inwardly they are ferocious wolves. By their fruit you will recognize them [. . .]
> —Jesus, Matthew 7:15-16

The fruit of Jehovah in the book of Revelation is war, famine, suffering, fear, corruption, death, and disease. The "Lamb" who deceptively posed as the Christ is the Wolf in "sheep's covering":

> The Lamb who was slain deserves to receive power, wealth, wisdom, strength, honor, glory, and praise.
> —Revelation 5:12

It is not Jesus who sought to acquire wealth and egotistical power and fame, but rather the Wolf who masqueraded as the Lamb. We are also told that it was the so-called "Lamb" who unleashed the four horsemen of the Apocalypse to bring hell on Earth. Therefore, it is likely that the author of the book of Revelation was in-league with the Wolf. In this case, it can be concluded that the author was one of the false prophets that Jesus warned his followers about.

Moreover, the "vision" that "John" claimed to have witnessed never actually happened. What the cunning author did was simply use Old Testament motifs in order to advance a Yahwehist agenda.

Despite Jesus's repeated warnings, the leaders of Paul's church failed to recognize the signs. One of the ways that this was able to happen was due to the unfortunate inability of the people to read, analyze, and interpret the scriptures for themselves. Because of this lack of education, the parochial laity were forced to trust Pauline officials—officials who never understood the true mission of Jesus to begin with!

Of course, the result of all of this deliberate deception and unintentional misunderstanding is that the forces of Jehovah prevailed.

> [. . .] See, the Lion of the tribe of Judah, the Root of David, has triumphed [. . .]
> —Revelation 5:5

In the following passage, the Wolf commends those who have kept his (Jehovah's) name, and rewards the obedient by offering to spare them from the horrors of the Tribulation:

> I know that you [the church of Philadelphia] have little strength, yet you have kept my word and have not denied my name [. . .] Since you have kept my command to endure patiently, I will also keep you from the hour of trial that is going to come upon the world to test those who live on the earth.
> —Revelation 3:8-10

Realizing what was actually happening, the gnostic Christians referred to this tragedy in the following passage:

> After he [Yaldabaoth] imprisoned those from the Father, he seized them and fashioned them to resemble himself. And it is with him that they exist.
> —Nag Hammadi Codices, The Second Apocalypse of James

A similar sentiment is found in the canonical account:

> When anyone hears the message about the kingdom and does not understand it, the evil one comes and snatches away what was sown in his heart [. . .]
> —Jesus, Matthew 13:19

Peter and Paul were the ones who heard the message but did not fully understand it. Because of their ignorance, the legacy of the Lord of Armies was able to not only survive but to advance. However, it is unlikely that this operation had been orchestrated by Yahweh himself, but rather by agents who had been conditioned to uphold his legacy. One of those agents was the author of the book of Revelation.

What the book of the Revelation of John documents is a massive Machiavellian operation that was intended to extend the power of the Lord of Armies outside the old Semitic realm. This new Machiavellian operation called for the affliction of the people of the world with disease, famine, and war, in order to "kill a third of mankind," before stepping in at a later time to present himself as their glorious benefactor:

> [. . .] And God will wipe away every tear from their eyes.
> —Revelation 7:17

Of course, this act of generous mercy was granted only on the condition that the people submit themselves as slaves that "serve him day and night":

> [. . .] the survivors were terrified and gave glory to the God
> of heaven.
> —Revelation 11:13

* * *

Many Paulines believe that the Apocalypse will be accompanied by the return of Jesus to the world. One of the sources that is used to justify this belief is found in Luke 21:27. In this passage, Jesus warns his followers about a future calamity. He warns that they may not survive the turmoil, and that they should be ready to meet him in the Kingdom of the Heavenly Father. In this case, Jesus was not literally returning to Earth in physical form, but rather was helping his followers to cross over to the other side upon their deaths from this unfortunate event.

In my Father's house are many homes. If it weren't so, I
would have told you. I am going to prepare a place for you.
If I go and prepare a place for you, I will come again, and
will receive you to myself; that where I am, you may be
there also.
—Jesus, John 14:2-3

Jesus told his followers that the Tribulation would occur in their own
generation:

Truly I tell you, this generation will certainly not pass away
until all these things have happened.
—Jesus, Mark 13:30

Therefore, the Tribulation was never supposed to occur in some
apocalyptic age in the far future, such as the present time—as is
commonly believed. For Paulines to disagree with this conclusion they
would have to disagree with the words that are actually recorded in the
Bible itself. Even the account that is documented in the book of
Revelation clearly indicates that the End Times were not thousands of
years in the future, but rather "near" and "soon":

Do not seal up the words of the prophecy of this scroll,
because the time is near.
—Revelation 22:10

Look, I am coming soon! [. . .]
—Revelation 22:12

Likewise, according to the New Testament letters, the "antichrist" was
predicted to arrive in the age in which it was written:

Children, it's the end of time. You've heard that an
antichrist is coming. Certainly, many antichrists are already
here. That's how we know it's the end of time.

It could be said that the destruction of Jerusalem and the apocalyptic Tribulation were fulfilled in AD 70, when the Romans attacked Jerusalem and destroyed the Temple of Yahweh. Indeed, in Mark 13:1 Jesus seems to predict the destruction of the Temple—that is, if we assume that this passage was not inserted by the author after the events had already occurred. It is also reported that during the Tribulation event, when Jerusalem was "surrounded by armies," the people would "flee to the mountains" (Luke 21:20-21); which did occur when the Jewish rebels fled to Masada in order to escape the Roman army.

The return of the Savior (i.e., *Parousia*) could either be the resurrection after the crucifixion, or perhaps more likely his spiritual manifestation in heaven—which is what Marcion[40] and the gnostics[41] believed. Indeed, according to Mark 12:25, Jesus indicated that the resurrection was not physical, but rather spiritual; which is also corroborated in 1 Corinthians 15:35-52. Therefore, Judgment Day is the event in which a soul ascends into the world of spirit after the death of the physical body; which would be an event that would be more frequent during the Tribulation. Those whose hearts and minds were pure would be able to ascend into the Kingdom of Heaven. This was also an event that was supposed to occur not thousands of years in the future, but rather during the time of Jesus; hence the following statement:

> [. . .] And you will see the Son of Man sitting at the right hand of the Mighty One and coming on the clouds of heaven.
> —Mark 14:62

In this case, references to a physical resurrection that appear in the New Testament may actually be revised interpretations that that were inserted by well-meaning devotees who were not present during the time of the actual events. Furthermore, it must be understood that it was the scribe's

---

40 The Panarion (i.e., Against Heresies) (Book I, part 42) by Epiphanius of Salamis.

41 The Sophia of Jesus Christ, Nag Hammadi codices.

duty to impress the reader and thereby inspire conversion to Judeo-Christianity. Expanding upon the supernatural element was a way in which to do this.

A primary reason why these passages that confirm the preterist[42] position have been ignored by many Paulines is because the belief that Armageddon, the Tribulation, the Rapture, the Apocalypse, and the return of the Christ are about to happen, infuses their belief system with an element of exciting faith-bolstering relevance. The other effect of this interpretation is that it compels fearful obedience for those who may be concerned about the horrendous adversity that is foretold, and about the horror of being "left behind" during the "Rapture"—which further acts to benefit the institution of Pauline Judeo-Christianity itself. However, the concept of the Rapture is based on yet another misunderstanding.

* * *

The concept of the Rapture is related to the Tribulation that is believed will occur during the apocalyptic End Times. Many Judeo-Christians believe that those who are faithful to Lord Jehovah will be taken up into heaven, while those who are not will be "left behind" to suffer the prophesized calamity. The biblical precedent for this belief is found in the following passages:

> Two men will be in the field; one will be taken and the other left. Two women will be grinding with a hand mill; one will be taken and the other left. Therefore keep watch, because you do not know on what day your Lord will come.
> —Jesus, Matthew 24:40-42

> But no one know of that day and hour, not even the angels of heaven, but my Father only.
> —Jesus, Matthew 24:36

---

42 Preterism is the belief that the events described in the book of Revelation have already happened.

[. . .] keep on the watch, therefore, because you know neither the say nor the hour.
—Jesus, Matthew 25:13

For the Lord himself will come down from heaven, with a loud command, with the voice of the archangel and with the trumpet call of God, and the dead in Christ will rise first. After that, we who are still alive and are left will be caught up together with them in the clouds to meet the Lord in the air. And so we will be with the Lord forever. Therefore encourage one another with these words.
—1 Thessalonians 4:16-18

According to the gospels, Jesus himself indicated that on that day a person's material possessions will no longer mean anything. The reason for this is because on that day that person will no longer be in the physical world because he or she would have ascended into the world of spirit. In the Gospel of Luke, where some of the alleged references to the Rapture occur, Jesus also makes a reference to a "dead body" (Luke 17:37). The original reason for the references to a dead body and to the end of material possessions is because what he was referring to was the death of the physical body. This is what the Rapture actually is. This is also what the "Day of Judgment" is as well.

The word "rapture" is a term that is found in the Latin Vulgate translation of the Bible. It is derived from the word *raeptis*, which means "taken away" or "caught up." This is a reference to someone's spirit form, or soul, being caught up and taken away into heaven, which is essentially a euphemistic term for death.

When these people, however, have completed the time of the kingdom and the spirit leaves them, their bodies will die but their souls will be alive, and they will be taken up.
—Jesus, The Gospel of Judas

80

When Jesus was referring to people who would be "taken up," it was a reference to those whose lives would be *taken*—that is, taken up out of the physical world and raptured into the realm of "everlasting life" in the spiritual world. What he was doing was advising the people to be mentally and spiritually prepared for that event.

This is something that Paul never fully understood; hence his statement in 1 Thessalonians 4:16-17, in which he differentiates between the dead and the living, who he says will both be taken up separately into the clouds with Jesus.

When Jesus talked about what has come to be known as the Rapture, he referred to when the people of Sodom had been killed in the fire of the Lord, which is another reference to death. According to Jesus, that was not the end of their lives, for they were resurrected into the realm of everlasting life in the spiritual world. In this case, the only ones who will be "left behind" are those who do not enter into the light after the expiration of their physical form.

Indeed, one of Jesus's primary aims was to make the people aware of the Kingdom of Heaven in the after-life. This is why he emphasized preparation by cultivating a virtuous psyche in this world. Up until that point, the emphasis in the Old Testament/Tanakh was mostly placed on an underworld state that is referred to as "Sheol," or "Gehenna," which are essentially Hebrew words for the grave and hell. Although, there were instances in which a joyous afterlife existence was alluded to (e.g., Isaiah 26:19; Daniel 12:2), these exceptions are both sparse and brief. The word translated as "heaven" or "the heavens" (*shamayim*) originally only referred to the firmament of the sky (e.g., Deuteronomy 28:12), not to the blissful "Kingdom of Heaven" in the after-life (*Basileia tou Ouranou*) that is referred to by Jesus (e.g., Luke 10:15).

* * *

Other misunderstandings in the book of Revelation relate to so-called "beasts," "serpents," leviathan "dragons," and the infamous "antichrist." However, what is commonly misunderstood about the term "antichrist" is that it does not even appear in the book of Revelation. This term actually only appears in the New Testament Epistles of John, who is not the author of Revelation. Of course, the "false prophet" of Revelation could be considered to be an antichrist, just as anyone who denies the significance of the Christ could be—which is the original definition of the term according to "John" himself. Indeed, this is why the term appears in plural form (1 John 2:18; 2 John 1:7). The book of Revelation indicates that the prophesied events would appear in their own generation, and it is in that generation that we will discover the identity of its characters.

In the latter half of the first century of the Common Era, the primary antagonists of the Christians were not only the Yahwehists but the Romans. The Romans were not only originally unreceptive to the religions of Yahweh/Jehovah but were also involved in self exultation and the worship of pagan gods. Therefore, the author of Revelation related Rome to the city of Babylon. There is even a cryptic reference to Rome in the following passage:

> This calls for a mind with wisdom. The seven heads [of the beast] are seven hills on which the woman [the Whore of Babylon] sits.
> —Revelation 17.9

The "seven hills" refers to the seven hills on which the city of Rome was built.[25] The following verse indicates that the "woman" represents the city of Rome itself:

> The woman you saw is the great city that rules over the kings of the earth.
> —Revelation 17:18

The hostile pagan Romans incarcerated the Christians and sentenced them to cruel deaths:

> I saw that the woman was drunk with the blood of God's holy people, the blood of those who bore testimony to Jesus.

—Revelation 17:6

The reason why Revelation was encrypted with symbolism was to conceal its message from the Roman authorities, who would have destroyed it along with anyone who possessed it.

In the following passage, we find a cryptic reference to a series of kings:

> This call for a mind with wisdom. The seven heads are seven hills on which the woman sits. They are also seven kings. Five have fallen, one is, the other has not yet come; but when he does come, he must remain for only a little while. The beast who once was, and now is not, is an eighth king. He belongs to the seven and is going to his destruction.
> —Revelation 17:9-11

The five who have fallen refers to the five Roman emperors of the Julio-Claudian dynasty who had ruled since the time Jesus was born—those emperors being: Augustus, Tiberius, Gaius (i.e., Caligula), Claudius, and Nero. The emperor "kings" who came after the first five were from the Flavian dynasty of Vespasian.[26] It was the eighth "king," Domitian, who sought to establish the formation of an imperial cult that was based on himself and the Flavian family that he descended from.[27] This bloodline included Vespasian and Titus; the very same Roman persecutors who were involved in the attack on the rebels in Judea. By establishing an imperial pagan institution with religious connotations that was hostile to Judeo-Christianity, Domitian had established himself as a "false prophet" in the mind of the author of Revelation.

The beast that is from the "earth" is either a high-priest of the imperial cult or a provincial governor, most likely in Asia Minor[28]—the same location where the churches mentioned in Revelation were located. This so-called "beast" made the people worship the image of the beast that is from the "sea." Both the "image" and the "mark" refer to monetary currency. We know this because in Revelation 13:17 we are told that they were linked to "buying" and "selling." Therefore, the mark is most likely a reference to an imperial seal (i.e., *charagma*) or a certificate of sacrifice (i.e., *libellus*). What this means is that the beast from the sea and his cohorts sought to control the wealth of the land. The Old Testament tells us that this was an indulgence that was reserved for Lord Yahweh (and his elite agents) alone. The "image" of the beast was the face of one of the emperors that appeared on the Roman coinage of the time. The "mark" is associated with the identity of the beast who is from the sea. This character is identified by the number "666." Scholars have discovered that by assigning numbers to the Hebrew alphabet using a numerology process known as gematria, that the numbers 666 can be derived from the words "Nero Caesar."[29] Therefore, the image that appeared on the currency was that of the Emperor Nero, who was an infamous persecutor of the early Christians. In this case, it can be concluded that Nero was the beast that came from the sea—namely, from out of the Mediterranean Sea from Rome. Indeed, it was Nero who initiated the Jewish-Roman Wars when he sent troops to quash the Great Revolt. It is highly likely that the author of Revelation was a refugee of that first war, which explains not only his exile to the island of Patmos but his Jewish Christian perspective.

According to Revelation 13:3, 13:14, the beast will be mortally wounded but will survive. This is another reference to Nero, who allegedly committed suicide but was thought to have survived.[30] Indeed, the return of Nero is known as the *Nero Redivivus* legend.[43]

The reality is that the "signs of the times" have always occurred and will continue to occur for years, centuries, and millennia to come. This is because the events and characters that are described in the book of Revelation are unintentionally infused with a fundamental archetypal significance that can be applied to a wide array of individuals and situations, including ones in the present day. However, it is now known that the situation that is referred to in the Apocalypse of John originally only applied to individuals and events that were occurring in the period in which it was written. This includes the character of the so-called

---

43 The Nero Redivivus legend is referred to in the book The City of God (Book XX) by Augustine of Hippo, and in the Sibylline Oracles (Book IV, V).

"antichrist." This is why, according to 1 John 4:2-3, the spirit of the antichrist is said to be "already in the world."

* * *

According to the book of Revelation, the war between the forces of good and evil will eventually bring about a new theocratic empire. The agents of the Lord of Armies were supposed to bring about this regime by the use of violence, oppression, deception, and fear. It could be said that what Revelation successfully predicted was the subsequent "Dark Ages." Indeed, the alliance that was made between the Paulines, the Roman Empire, and the barbarian tribes (more on this subject to come), put the power structure in place that enabled the forces of the Lord of Armies to inadvertently bring about the apocalyptic scenario that is described in the book of Revelation. Consequently, the age that followed can be associated with the four horsemen of the Apocalypse. It was a time of war, famine, death, disease, and the attainment of power and wealth by an elite and ruthless few. It is no coincidence that the rise of Christendom, and the apocalyptic Tribulation that followed, corresponds precisely with the time-frame of the medieval Dark Ages. Therefore, the Apocalypse was not the end of the world, but rather the end of an age.

A trend in recent scholarship is to restrict what was previously referred to as the Dark Ages—which is now usually referred to as the Early Middle Ages—to about the years AD 500 to AD 1000. This period is characterized by a decrease in information and civilization. However, a definition of "darkness" should be expanded to include the increase in repression, wars, famine, plague, and corruption that occurred during that time. Indeed, the brevity of this reduced time-frame leaves out some of the darkest moments in European history—which was the region that was the most effected. Not only did most of the infamous wars of the time— which is the "white horse" of the Apocalypse—not begin until the eleventh century but the Black Death/bubonic plague—which is the "pale horse" of the Apocalypse—did not fully occur until the fourteenth century. The Paulines were also able to acquire a good deal of wealth from the spoils of conquest—which is the "black horse" of the

Apocalypse. All of those wars, plagues, and abuses of power, led to sporadic food shortages due to lost crops. The resulting famine was the "red horse" of the Apocalypse. It was also during that period that the atrocities of the Inquisitions occurred. Not only were the alleged enemies of Jehovah imprisoned in dungeons and executed but many were subjected to horrific acts of torture—in much the same way that the so-called "wicked" will be judged and punished during the Apocalypse.

Despite all of the tribulations that occurred after the year AD 1000, many historians are satisfied with the truncated time-line; however, the region that was most effected by this especially tumultuous period did not actually begin to see the light until the time of the Renaissance (from the French word for "rebirth") in the fifteenth and sixteenth centuries; as well as the following Age of Enlightenment. Indeed, the original Dark Ages coincided with the Middle Ages—which is the period between the fall of Rome and the Renaissance. This is the most accurate time-frame. Therefore, ideally, the medieval Dark Ages should be classified as the Early and Late Dark Ages. Moreover, it can be contended that the "Dark Ages" moniker still applies.

It is true that Renaissance type movements did occur during the Middle Ages. The Carolingian Renaissance, of the eighth and ninth centuries, was the first of three cultural revivals. However, these revivals were not only limited to the rediscovery of literature from the Roman Pauline empire of the fourth century AD but the effects of the rebirth were mostly limited to the clergy and the literate elite. Likewise, the Ottonian Renaissance of the tenth century was also limited in its scope and impact. The closest movement that could be described as a true cultural revival was perhaps the Twelfth Century Renaissance; but even that was more of a precursor of things to come.

The turning point in this time-line should be marked by the invention of the printing press in AD 1450. This invention allowed the mass production of information, which made it more possible for the public to read, learn, and think for themselves—which in turn led to subsequent progressive movements. Indeed, one of the books that was published during that time was the Bible. (It was also during that time that Niccolo Machiavelli's books were first printed.) Therefore, the entire Dark Ages actually lasted from the fifth to fifteenth centuries. Perhaps it is only coincidence that this is the thousand-year period of the reign of Jehovah that is predicted in the book of Revelation.[44]

It was also during that time that the pagan Eleusis festival in Greece was shut down. The last remnants of the Eleusian mysteries were eradicated in AD 396, when barbarian Goths, under the leadership of Alaric, who himself was an Arian Pauline, invaded Greece. The historian and Neo-Platonist philosopher Eunapius reports[45] that Alaric was accompanied by Christian monks "clad in black raiment." According to Eunapius, the monks were "tyrants" who showed "contempt for things divine," and "allowed countless unspeakable crimes." It was also during that same period that the Pauline emperor Theodosius 1 ordered the ban on the Olympic games, since it was also perceived as a pagan festival.

The Dark Ages are commonly blamed on the barbarians who attacked and destroyed Rome, thus bringing to an end the most advanced civilization of the ancient era—that is, despite its many ethical shortcomings. However, what is not commonly known is that the barbarians themselves were Judeo-Christians! The Visigoths, the Ostrogoths, the Vandals, as well as other smaller tribes, were all Pauline Judeo-Christians.[3146] The Germanic barbarians (as opposed to the Huns, who rejected the Paulines) had been converted to Judeo-Christianity by missionaries[47] even before the raid of Rome.[32]

* * *

Between the years AD 325 and 451, four Catholic Church councils were convened. It was these councils that developed a doctrine by which all others were to be considered heresy. One of the ways that they were able

---

44 In Revelation 20:3, it is reported that the adversary of Jehovah, who is likened to a "dragon," will be cast into the abyss for one thousand years to keep him from "deceiving" the nations. During that thousand-year period, the theocracy of Jehovah would prevail.

45 Lives of the Philosophers

46 Most were Arian Judeo-Christians. Arianism (attributed to the presbyter, Arius) is the belief that Jesus was not God himself, but rather the son of God (which is affirmed in John 14:28).

47 The most influential of which was the bishop, Ulfilas.

to control mental perspective was to destroy books that documented different viewpoints.

The book burning of the Pauline era began when the followers of Paul burned scrolls that were said to deal with "sorcery" (Acts 19:19). Likewise, Emperor Constantine ordered the burning of the book titled *Against the Christians* (written by the third-century Greek scholar and Neo-Platonist Philosopher Porphyry of Tyre). The same book was also burned by the Pauline emperors Valentinian II and Theodosius II.[33] (Porphyry himself was also physically assaulted by the Paulines.) The Catholic emperor Jovian ordered the burning of an entire library in Antioch.[34] Also in the fourth century, the theologian Arius was denounced by Constantine's first Council of Nicaea because of his views pertaining to Jesus and the Father; and as a result his books were destroyed.[35] The decree against Arian Christian writings was also made by the Catholic Visigoth king Reccared, in the sixth century.[36] In the thirteenth century, the Roman Catholic Paulines burned the books of the Christian Cathars.[37] It was in that same century that the library of Constantinople was destroyed by Roman Catholic crusaders.[38] In the thirteenth and fourteenth centuries, the Roman Catholics burned thousands of Jewish books (e.g., the works of Maimonides and the Talmud, etc.).[39] In the fifteenth century, the writings of the Judeo-Christian reformist John Wycliffe were banned and burned by order of the Roman Catholic Church.[40] Also in the fifteenth century, the Spanish inquisitor Tomas de Torquemada ordered the burning of non-Roman Catholic approved literature.[41] It was around this same time that the Pauline cardinal Cisneros ordered that the books of the Nasrid library in Granada Spain be removed and burned.[42] In the sixteenth century, the Spanish bishop Diego de Landa and his accomplices burned the codices of the Maya in the Yucatan.[43] It was around this same time that missionaries destroyed Buddhist texts in Japan.[44] Also in the sixteenth century, all books written in the native Sanskrit and Marathi languages were burned by the agents of the Inquisition in the Portuguese colony of Goa, no matter what the subject matter.[45] One of the first known cases of book burning committed by Protestant Paulines occurred in 1520, when Martin Luther burned the theologian Angelo Carletti di Chivasso's book *Summa de Casibus*

Conscientiae, along with other papal literature.[46] Likewise, Protestants burned the Italian theologian Francesco Stancaro's book *Collatio doctrinae Arii* (etc.).[47] These are only a few examples of the extensive destruction and repression that occurred.[48]

Although it is true that non-Judeo-Christians were also guilty of committing similar transgressions, it should be understood that Judeo-Christendom was not always the great guardian benefactor of civilization that is commonly proclaimed by the Paulines.

During the Dark Ages, the Roman Catholic Paulines ruled with an iron hand. If a supposed "heretic" was repentant he would only have his books burned and he would be forced to publicly recant. The unfortunate ones were either imprisoned for life or sentenced to death. Some who received the death penalty were strangled before their bodies were burned at the stake. Others were slowly burned alive.[48] Indeed, many were

---

48 The following is a list of some prominent intellectuals whose work was also banned by the Paulines: The theologian Ratramnus of Corbu (1050); The philosopher Berengar of Tours (1050); The philosopher, theologian, and logician Peter Abelard (1121, 1140); The philosopher Almaric (Amaury) of Bene (1210); The philosopher and theologian David of Dinant (1210); The philosopher Johannes Scotus Erigena (John the Scot) (1225); The rabbi and philosopher Maimonides (1233); The Judeo-Christian reformist Gerard Segarelli (1300); The theologian Petrus Johannes Oliva (Peter Olivi) (1328); The poet Dante Alighieri (1329); The physician, encyclopaedist, and professor Cecco d'Ascoli (1328); The philosopher, priest, and university rector John Hus (1415); The poet, astrologer/astronomer, and historian Don Enrique de Aragon (Marquis de Villa) (1434); The professor Pedro Martinez de Osma (1481); The physician and astrologer/astronomer Simon de Phares (1494); The humanist and lawyer Johannes Reuchlin (1514); The humanist and translator Louis de Berquin (1523); The French scholar and printer Etienne Dolet (1546); The Protestant reformer Martin Bucer (1555); The political philosopher Jean Bodin (1591); The philosopher, mathematician, and astrologer/astronomer Giordano Bruno (1599); The poet Agrippa d'Aubigne (1620); The poet Theophile de Viau (1623); The theologian Ferninando de las Infantes (1605); The scientist Marco Antonio de Dominis (1624); The physician Francisco Maldonado de Silva (1639); The theologian Jonas Schlichting (1646); The Unitarian reformer John Biddle (1647, 1655); The mathematician, physicist, inventor, and philosopher Blaise Pascal (1657, 1660); The political philosopher Thomas Hobbes (1683); The theologian and rector of Exeter College at Oxford Arthur Bury (1690); The philosopher John Toland (1697); The historian Pietro Giannone (1723); The philosopher and writer Voltaire (1734, 1759 etc.); The philosopher and writer Denis Diderot (1746, 1759); The philosopher, musician, and writer Jean Jacques Rousseau (1762, 1764 etc.). Note: Even more cases are cited in Haig Bosmajian's *Burning Books* (2006).

burned at the stake together with their books. Furthermore, not only were authors arrested and killed but booksellers and printers as well.[49] A papal bull issued by Pope Leo X stated that books could not be printed until they passed a rigorous inspection process by ecclesiastical censors.[50] During the Spanish Inquisition, manuscripts were also required to be reviewed by censors. (i.e., the Censorship Law of 1558), and all printing had to be licensed by a bishop.[51] In England, no printing was allowed outside of Cambridge, Oxford, and London.[52] Thousands of books were also confiscated and destroyed at Oxford in 1535 and 1550.[53] Because church and state were linked, the book burning was extended to not only heretical writings but anything that could be interpreted to be "seditious."[54] Consequently, private homes and private libraries were also raided. For example, in Spain, the books in the library of the Marquis of Villena were seized and burned in 1434.[55] Moreover, in the sixteenth century the List of Prohibited Books (*Index Librorum Prohibitorum*) was created in order to suppress free speech and thought.

The following quote that is attributed to Jesus could have been addressed to those censors of free speech:

> Woe to you experts in the law, because you have taken away the key to knowledge. You yourselves have not entered, and you have hindered those who were entering.
> —Yeshua, Luke 11:52

Although some classical works of literature were collected and preserved in Catholic monastery libraries, in some cases these documents were erased in order to make way for Pauline literature. This was a practice known as palimpsesting. An example of this is the Archimedes palimpsest, in which the works of one of the greatest mathematic minds of the ancient world was erased and written over by a Catholic scribe who needed a writing surface (i.e., vellum) on which he could record liturgical text.[56]

In the sixteenth century, the English scholar William Tyndale translated the Bible directly from early Greek and Hebrew texts. The result was not only an edition that was more accurate than the official

Latin Vulgate edition that had been sanctioned by the Catholic Church, but a Bible that was more accessible to the public, since it was written in the common language of the day. However, his translations were not considered favorable to the Catholic Church, since, among other reasons, he used words such as "congregation" instead of church, and "senior" instead of priest. Therefore, his Bible was confiscated and he was strangled to death before his corpse was burned at the stake.[57] Despite his demise, his ground-breaking translations became the foundation of the popular King James Bible that is still in use to this day—although, it should be understood that even this edition cannot be considered to be entirely accurate.[58]

* * *

The Pauline Roman emperors saw themselves as existing above the common morality of man, since their authority was thought to be ordained by God. It was a position that was recommended by Machiavelli in the following passage:

> And in fact, there was never anyone who ordained new and unusual laws among the people without having recourse to God, for they would not otherwise have been accepted. This is so because prudent men know of many beneficial things which, having no persuasive evidence for them, they cannot get others to accept. Consequently, wise men who wish to avoid this difficulty resort to divine authority.
> —Niccolo Machiavelli, *Discourses on Livy*

One of the advantages of combining the affairs of church and state is that it can be used to justify war. Soldier martyrs were promised eternal rewards for those who gave up their lives in service to the "Creator." As a result, a great many pious followers died while following the orders of rulers who they were led to believe were inspired by "God." During the Crusades, for example, the Roman Catholic soldiers believed that they were fighting not only for the liberation of the Holy Land but for the remission of sin;[59] even though the "Holy Wars" themselves were brutally violent events in which looting and rape occurred (e.g., the sack of Constantinople).[60] Eventually, the lure of acquiring wealth also became a factor as new markets opened up and donations and pillaging helped to enrich the Roman Catholic Church.[61]

The Pauline sect developed a dogmatic creed that was not only based on the death of the Christ and servitude to Jehovah but emphasized the fear-based threat of eternal damnation. The laity were also led to believe that to follow Jesus was to embrace the meek and mild mentality of a suffering martyr, which was an interpretation that further acted to weaken and subdue the people.

> If our religion claims of us fortitude of soul, it is more to enable us to suffer than to achieve great deeds. These principles seem to me to have made men feeble, and caused them to become an easy prey to evil-minded men, who can control them more securely, seeing that the great body of men, for the sake of gaining paradise, are more disposed to endure injuries than to avenge them.
> —Niccolo Machiavelli, *Discourses on Livy*

Church officials were also able to deflect criticism directed at themselves and the situations that the suffering laity found themselves in by redirecting blame onto an adversarial devil scapegoat; even though the book of Revelation tells us that it was the will of Jehovah himself to inflict the world with tribulation.

> So simple-minded are men and so controlled by immediate necessities, that a prince who deceives always finds men who let themselves be deceived.
> —Niccolo Machiavelli, *The Prince*

During the apocalyptic age, widespread corruption in the highest levels of the church took place as various Roman Catholic officials jockeyed among themselves for power, prestige, and wealth. Some high-ranking positions could even be bought for a nominal sum—a practice known as "Simony."[49] Even though Simony was officially condemned by the Roman Catholic Church, it was a widespread practice in the ninth and tenth centuries.[62]

Another problem that resulted was the continuation of a sexist male-dominated power system (see also 1 Corinthians 14:34-35).

> A woman should learn in quietness and full submission.
> —1Timothy 2:11

To this day, women are forbidden from holding any high positions—especially in the Catholic Church.

> Thus we must conclude, that a husband is meant to rule over his wife as the spirit rules over the flesh.
> —Augustine of Hippo,[50] *City of God*

* * *

It is commonly believed that Judeo-Christendom was a beacon of light in the Dark Ages. While it is true that some Paulines did actually follow the example that was established by Jesus, such as Saint Francis of Assisi and the other great lesser-known altruistic saints of the time, the fact is that the rise of that oppressive and tumultuous age in human history coincides with the rise of Judeo-Christendom.

It is true that hospitals and universities were constructed by the Paulines; however, during that time hospitals were more devoted to care rather than to cures. Even though limited attempts were made into the study of medicine, diseases were also often thought to be the punishment inflicted on sinners by God—especially before the emergence of the natural philosophers, which did not occur until the late Dark Ages. Holy relics and icons were also sometimes used in an attempt to ward off

---

49 A reference to Simon Magus, who, according to Acts 8:18, attempted to purchase the ability to heal from the apostles.

50 Augustine was an influential fifth-century Pauline theologian, philosopher, and bishop of Hippo.

illnesses as a greater emphasis was placed on faith rather than reason.[63] Philosophical inquiry and rational thought were discouraged by such prominent Catholic archbishops as Gregory Nazianzus and John Chrysostom.[64] It was not until the end of the Dark Ages that breakthroughs in health care were made by scientists, such as the microbiologist Antonie van Leeuwenhoek, and the polymath Michael Servetus—who nevertheless was sentenced to death by the Paulines, both Catholic and Protestant, due to differences that pertained to theological interpretations.[65]

The truth is that hospitals existed even before the rise of Judeo-Christendom. Some of the first hospitals were built by the Greeks, as well as the Indian and Sri Lankan Buddhists in the third and fourth centuries BC.[66][67] The ancient Egyptians also created medical treatises, such as the Ebers Papyrus, circa 1550 BC,[68] and what has come to be referred to as the Edwin Smith Papyrus, circa 1600 BC—although there is evidence that this document had been copied from older texts that date back to the Old Kingdom period, circa 3000 BC.[69] Furthermore, the earliest attempt at a pharmacopoeia, in the form of a Sumerian written tablet, also dates back to the third millenium BC.[70]

Although monasteries, convents, and cathedral schools provided educational services during the Dark Ages, the curriculum was significantly limited. The Catholic cathedral schools in particular were focused primarily on religious instruction. Indeed, most of the students were male children of nobility who were preparing for careers in the church.

It is also true that the works of the philosopher Aristotle were preserved—that is, preserved from destruction by the Paulines themselves. It should also be remembered that it was a Pauline emperor (i.e., Justinian I) who initially shut down the last philosophic Academy. It is also disingenuous for Pauline traditionalists to claim that the Judeo-Christians were the leading scholars of the age when they forcefully silenced other voices. Although the Judeo-Christian Paulines are usually credited with preserving the works of Aristotle during the Middle Ages, there were also times when the Paulines (e.g., the Dominicans)[51]

---

51 The Dominicans are a Roman Catholic organization that was founded in the

condemned Aristotle and ordered his writings to be burned.[71] Furthermore, in 1210 an edict was issued by a Catholic synod at the University of Paris that forbid lecturing on the subject of Aristotelian metaphysics and natural science.[72] In 1231, Pope Gregory IX ordered that Aristotle's writings could not be reinstated until all offending errors in his works were removed.[73] In 1245, Pope Innocent IV extended the ban to the University of Toulouse.[74] Likewise, acting on a request by Pope John XXI, the bishop of Paris, Stephen Tempier, issued an edict in 1277 that prohibited the teaching of 219 theological and philosophical works at the University of Paris that he deemed to be heretical.[75]

The sixteenth-century astronomer Nicolaus Copernicus was at first unable to publish the discovery that the Earth revolved around the sun, because the findings contradicted the Pauline belief in an Earth-centered universe. Therefore, he did not release his findings until he was near the end of his life. Indeed, Copernicus was condemned by the Dominican theologian and astrologer Giovanni Maria Tolosani, who believed—among other false assumptions—that mathematics could not be used to calculate activities in the natural world;[76] although mathematics is now the primary tool that is used by physicists.

However, it was not only the Catholics who were impeding progress. The Protestant theologian Philipp Melanchthon—who was Martin Luther's primary collaborator, also called for Copernicus's theory to be repressed by governmental force.[77]

> [. . .] certain people believe it is a marvelous achievement to extol so crazy a thing, like that Polish astronomer who makes the earth move and the sun stand still. Really, wise governments ought to repress impudence of mind.
> —Philipp Melanchthon, Letter to Mithobius

The Protestant theologian John Owen also condemned the works of Copernicus. He declared that the heliocentric theory was based on "fallible phenomena" that contradicted the "testimonies of Scripture."[78] Likewise, the following statement was written by the Protestant-

---

thirteenth century.

influenced Pauline theologian, John Calvin:

> We indeed are not ignorant that the circuit of the heavens is
> finite, and that the earth, like a little globe, is placed in the
> center.
> —John Calvin, *Commentaries of the First Book of Moses*
> *called Genesis*

Although Copernicus managed to avoid any serious consequences, in
1663 Galileo Galilei was convicted of heresy for similar findings and was
placed under house arrest by the Roman Catholic Paulines for the rest of
his life.

* * *

During the Pauline Dark Ages, free thought was repressed and the
academic curriculum was restricted. It was the humanists that helped to
unrestrict it. Humanism was a movement that promoted rationalism,
empiricism, ethics, and science. Although the first humanists were a small
progressive faction within the Pauline institution, over the centuries the
movement became increasingly secular. It was the Humanists who
transformed the universities into the institutions of higher learning that
we know today.

> Humanism drove much of the curricular and research
> innovation. After joining university faculties, humanists
> transformed the study of grammar and rhetoric into the
> *studia humanitatis*. Once humanistic studies and humanists
> became established in the university, scholars in other
> disciplines acquired their philological and linguistic
> expertise, along with the humanistic ideology that viewed
> ancient texts as the true source of learning, and medieval
> scholarship as a barrier to them. Humanistically inclined
> scholars changed the content of instruction and research in
> all disciplines except theology.

—P. F. Grendler, *The Universities of the Italian Renaissance*

What is less commonly known is that some of the first universities were initially independent from Judeo-Christendom. Indeed, the world's first university, the University of Bologna (founded in 1088), was initially a student-run institution that was independent of both kings and popes.

It is true that the founding of these institutions, or simply allowing the secular universities to exist, was a step in the right direction; however, both students and teachers were required to operate under limiting regulations. Indeed, the pioneering seventeenth-century philosopher Rene Descartes cautiously remarked[52] that the people of his time were more influenced by custom than by genuine knowledge of the truth.

It should also be understood that the Pauline wars, such as the Thirty Years' War, disrupted the progress that was being made by the universities.

* * *

It was also during that period that the Roman Catholics engaged in the selling of "indulgences," which was money paid to the church for the remission of the punishments for sin. A percentage of what little money, or grain, animals, etc., that the peasant class did possess, was forced back into the church coffers in the form of "tithes." It was also during that time that the Roman Catholic armies would sweep through the lands and either kill or heavily tax its inhabitants. Of course, all of this would have appalled Jesus.

> For what does it profit a man if he gains the whole world,
> and loses or forfeits his own self?
> —Jesus, Luke 9:25

In the thirteenth century, a series of battles that were directed against a tribe of peasants in northern Germany (i.e., the Stedingers) were launched

---

52 *Meditations on First Philosophy*

by both the Archbishop of Bremen and Pope Gregory IX. The war began after the peasants refused to perform forced labor and pay tithes to the archbishop. Despite some early success, the peasants were eventually violently suppressed.[79]

Jewish people were targeted because they denied that Jesus was the Mashiach. In 1391, the Spanish cleric and Archdeacon of Ecija in Seville, Ferrand Martinez, instigated a "Holy War" against the Jews for blasphemy. Those who did not convert were slaughtered.[80] The persecution of the Jews (i.e., "pogroms") throughout the centuries included not only expulsions and forced conversions but outright massacres (e.g., the Rhineland Massacre of 1096; the Strasbourg Massacre of 1349; the Lisbon Massacre of 1506; etc.).

Likewise, over a millenium earlier, the Roman Catholic emperor Theodosius I sentenced the gnostic Manichaens, along with other smaller Christian sects (i.e., Encratites; Saccophores; Hydroparastates), to death.[81] Other Pauline emperors (i.e., Justin and Justinian) initiated similar campaigns, until the Manichaens were also struck down.[82]

The Medieval Inquisitions (e.g., the Episcopal Inquisition, etc.) were initiated in 1184 by Pope Lucius III. Likewise, Pope Gregory IX authorized the Papal Inquisition in 1233. In 1478, the atrocities of the Spanish Inquisition began. It was during that period that censorship and the burning of books intensified. The result was a decline not only in freedom but in intellectual achievement.[83] Other Inquisitions included the Roman Inquisition, the Portugese Inquisition, and the Goa Inquisition, etc.

Just as Jesus had been convicted of heresy by the priests of Jehovah, so did Pauline officials sentence "heretics" to death for the crime of disobeying the will of Jehovah.

> [. . .] Beware of the yeast of the pharisees, which is hypocrisy.
> —Jesus, Luke 12:1

It can therefore be concluded that the form of Christianity that the world has become familiar with was not successful because it was the most truthful, but rather because it was the most oppressive and violent.

* * *

Throughout the Inquisitions, torture occurred in dark underground dungeons. During the torture sessions, an inquisitor, or some other commissioner of the Holy Office, would be present to act as overseers. The torture itself was carried out by men clad in black who often wore masks.

Torture was first authorized by Pope Innocent IV in 1252, and amended in 1256 by Pope Alexander IV. Alexander's addition authorized inquisitors to absolve one another of transgressions (i.e., "irregularities") that might occur while carrying out their duties.[84]

Torture instruments that were used by the inquisitors included the *strappado*, which was a rope and pulley device that hoisted victims who were suspended by their hands behind their backs up into the air before letting them down in quick jerking movements that inflicted horrible pain and damage.[85] Some were choked with water,[86] while others suffered upon the rack; which was a device that separated bones from their joints by pulling the feet and arms in opposite directions.[87] Another practice was the ordeal by fire, in which the victim was strapped down and fire was held to his or her feet.[88] The torture was not supposed to last more than the time it took to recite a prayer, and was not supposed to last more than a single session; however, these rules were not always heeded.[89] If the victim confessed to heresy, the confession had to be repeated outside the torture chamber. If the victim refused to confirm the confession, he or she might be sent back and tortured again.[90] Children were not spared and were subjected to painful interrogation practices as well.[91] There were also sadists among the torturers, who stripped their victims naked before abusing them.[92] One of the primary aims was not only to inflict pain and terror but to denigrate and humiliate their victims until the ordeal could no longer be tolerated and the desired confession was obtained.[93] The Roman Catholic Paulines were also able to profit from their activities by seizing the property of alleged "heretics."[94]

It is unknown for sure how many people were imprisoned, injured, and killed by the Inquisitions; just as it is also unknown how many innocent victims falsely confessed to heresy only as a means of ending their ordeal. It is known, however, that many victims were condemned based only on circumstantial evidence.[95]

In recent times, some individuals, who are often affiliated with the Catholic Church, have attempted to soften the atrocities that were committed during that period. Despite such blatant revisionism, it should be understood that it is evidential fact that crimes against humanity were indeed perpetrated by the servants of Jehovah during the Dark Ages.

Some of the physical persecution lasted all the way up until the 1700s, in the form of witch hunts—many of which were committed by the Protestant Paulines. The peak witch-hunting years occurred in Germany in the sixteenth and seventeenth centuries. A conservative estimate of the number of people who were killed for alleged witchcraft by the Paulines during that period is 45,000.[96]

The Paulines not only attacked anything related to paganism but mysticism as well, since it was believed that anything pertaining to the supernatural that was not in the Bible was the devil's sorcery. Of course, these were the same type of charges that were directed at Jesus when he was performing miracles as well:

> And the teachers of the law who came down from Jerusalem said, "He is possessed by Beelzebul! By the prince of demons he is driving out demons."
> —Mark 3:22

The irony and the error of the situation went unrealized by the Paulines, and as a result, their oppressive law prevailed.

> Our first debt to the Church and her priests is that, thanks to them, we Italians have become irreligious and wicked. But we owe it a still greater debt—the second cause of our ruin: that is, that the Church has kept and still keeps this country divided.

The Paulines brought about more adversity when missionaries entered into other sovereign regions around the world. They brought with them not only their mistaken interpretations of the Bible but their physical diseases as well. Although it is true that horrible indigenous practices, such as human sacrifice, were eradicated, in many cases the missionaries also banned harmless activities and set up a repressive imperialist church system that instilled "the fear of God" into the people.

* * *

In the twelfth century, gnostic Christianity reemerged in the form of the Cathars (or *Kathari,* which means "Pure Ones"). According to the Cistercian monk Raynaldus,[53] one of the Cathari blasphemies was that they believed that the Roman Catholic Church was corrupt.

The Cathars (also known as the Albigenses) were related to the Bogomiles in Bulgaria. Both of these movements appear to have been inspired by the Manichean gnostics of third-century Persia. Another dualist[54] group that arose during that period were the Paulicians, who were also violently persecuted.

The Roman Catholic Paulines eventually recommenced its war on the resurgent gnostic Christians. One of the ways that they were able to do this was by offering freedom from eternal damnation, as well as the material incentive of land, to the loyal servants of Jehovah who fought against the Cathars.[97] In the war that followed (i.e., the Albigensian Crusades), hundreds of thousands of people, including woman and children, were slaughtered.

These types of uprisings continued sporadically throughout the years. Each time they were struck down by the Roman Catholic army. As a result, the Pauline faction continued to dominate as the gnostic Christians were once again forcefully suppressed.

---

53 *On the Accusations Against the Albigensians*

54 Dualism, in this context, is the belief in the existence of two different deities. The first is the spiritual true God of light, which can be associated with the heavenly Father of Jesus. The other is the lower level Demiurge, which is Yahweh.

* * *

In 1302, Pope Boniface VIII declared his absolute authority over all human beings:

> Therefore, we declare, state, define, and pronounce that it is altogether necessary to salvation for every human creature to be subject to the Roman pontiff.
> —Pope Boniface VIII, *Unum Sanctum*

In the twelfth century, the Augustinian reformer and monastery prior Arnold of Brescia was hanged and burned, and his writings were destroyed after he denounced the Catholic Church's materialism and advocated for greater liberty. Likewise, in 1600 the brilliant hermetic philosopher and astrologer Giordano Bruno was burned alive for, among other reasons, believing that the universe was populated with planetary worlds other than our own (i.e., the "plurality of worlds"). The only person who barely managed to escape with his life for disagreeing with the Roman Catholics was the Pauline reformist, Martin Luther.

Although the intention of the Protestant movement was certainly well-meaning, it was also a Christian movement that had nothing to do with dualistic gnostic knowledge—that is, in regard to the difference between Yahweh and the Father. The result was a creed that was about as equally flawed as its predecessor. Like the Catholic Paulines before him, Luther also did not understand the underlying truth of the mission of the Savior; and as a result, the mistake that was committed by the Catholics was carried over into the Protestant Reformation.

Luther may have been inspired by the Old Testament Lord of Armies when he exhorted his followers to kill thousands of rebellious peasants who were fighting for equality and human rights in feudalistic Europe during the German Peasants' War.[98] Although it is commonly believed that Luther deplored violence, he actually did condone such actions when he believed that it was necessary to crush those who were operating "outside the law of God and Empire."

Therefore let everyone who can, smite, slay, and stab, secretly or openly, remembering that nothing can be more poisonous, hurtful, or devilish than a rebel [. . .]
—Martin Luther, *Against the Murderous, Thieving Hordes of Peasants*

Luther also approved of the executions of the members of a Judeo-Christian reformist group known as the Anabaptists,[99] whose only major difference with the Lutherans, besides their pacifism, was that they believed in adult baptism, as opposed to infant baptism. Luther referred to the Anabaptists as "brainsick" "bastards," whose "parents were all adulterers and whoremongers."[55] Luther not only advocated for a policy of submission (i.e., serfdom) to the masters of the world, both religious and secular, but was also severe in his attitude toward the Jews, who he described as "poisonous bitter worms."[56] Luther even advocated for setting synagogues on fire and destroying Jewish homes. In his book *On the Jews and their Lies*, he stated that Jews should be prevented from teaching "on pain of life and limb." His hateful diatribes helped to instigate the violent persecution of Jews in Germany.

In the sixteenth century, the Protestant-influenced theologian John Calvin began his career in Switzerland when he spear-headed a movement that maligned free will and reserved salvation solely for an elite predestined "elect" (i.e., "unconditional election"). Those who were not fortunate enough to be born with such a status were destined for damnation (i.e., "reprobation"). Calvin based his interpretation on the premise that God controls every aspect of his creation and therefore does not leave anything to free will or chance. What is especially peculiar about this deterministic interpretation is that it not only contradicts scientific findings that prove the existence of randomness and uncertainty in nature but also passages in the Bible itself, where Jehovah clearly did not have foreknowledge of events (e.g., Genesis 3:9, etc.).

Calvin also played a part in the death of the theologian, physician, and

55 *A Commentary on Saint Paul's Epistle to the Galatians*
56 *On the Jews and Their Lies*

Renaissance humanist Michael Servetus, who he condemned as a heretic. Likewise, he also ordered that Servetus's book (*Christianismi Restitutio*) be burned. Indeed, the Calvinists sentenced other books to the flames as well.[100]

The Puritans were an Old Testament-based Calvinist offshoot sect who believed that humanity was inherently contaminated and in need of strict Judeo-Christian guidance. Sexuality was repressed, attendance at church was mandatory, and questioning the Bible was prohibited. Punishments included: fines, public shaming, imprisonment, whippings, and executions. In 1684, Puritan ministers published a book titled *An Arrow Against Profane and Promiscuous Dancing, drawn out of the Quiver of the Scriptures*. Of course, all of these oppressive rules actually contradicted the original spirit of the Savior. Jesus himself would have been appalled by such heartless small-mindedness.

> We played music for you, but you did not dance [. . .]
> —Jesus, Matthew 11:17

> When you strip without being ashamed, and you take your clothes and put them under your feet like little children and trample them, then [you] will see the son of the living one and you will not be afraid.
> —Jesus, The Gospel of Thomas, Nag Hammadi Codices

The Puritans were also the same sect that engaged in the witch hunts of the 1690s, in which over a hundred people were arrested and imprisoned —some of whom were tortured and killed. The Puritan theocracy that was established in the New World of America justified torture and persecuted not only people who they thought were pagans but non-Puritan Christians, such as the Quakers, as well.

The European "Wars of Religion" began in the sixteenth century and lasted for over a hundred years (e.g., the German Peasants' War; the War at Kappel; the Schmalkaldic War; the Eighty Years' War; the French Wars of Religion; the Thirty Years' War; the Wars of the Three Kingdoms; etc.). Some of these wars, such as the French Wars of Religion, were known for their brutal massacres (e.g., the Massacre of Vassy; the Saint Bartholomew Day Massacre; the Massacre of Merindol).

As a result of all of the Pauline infighting that occurred in Europe during the Thirty Years' War, many peasant farmers who were caught in the middle lost their crops, and after decades of warfare, plague, and starvation, the population of Germany dropped by approximately 25% to 40%.[101]

It was during that time that the Puritan "New Model Army" arose in England, Ireland, and Scotland. Its leader, Oliver Cromwell, cited Old Testament passages in order to justify his ruthless campaigns.

* * *

The Roman Catholic Paulines were aware of the power that the arts (i.e., aesthetics) had on the hearts and the minds of the people. They sought to control this power by establishing rules related to permissible artistic expression, and by soliciting the most talented artists of the day to promote their own interpretation of Christianity[57]—especially during the Counter Reformation.[102]

The word aesthetic is derived from the Greek word *aisthetikos* (i.e., *aisthanomai*), which essentially means "to perceive." The definition of the word relates to the ability of beauty to effect the perception of the observer.

The Roman Catholic Paulines commissioned monumental works of architecture in the form of majestic cathedrals that were intended to impress upon the observer the majesty and glory of not only Jehovah but of the institution of the Catholic Church itself. However, not even the power of Pauline Judeo-Christendom could stop the inevitable rise of the Renaissance that appeared at the end of the Dark Ages.

The Renaissance began in Florence Italy in the fifteenth century. It was a movement that not only promoted the humanistic genius of man but drew inspiration from pre-Judeo-Christian art and knowledge as well. The Renaissance also helped lead the way for the following Scientific

---

57 The need for an orthodox artistic standard was affirmed at the Council of Trent in the sixteenth century.

Revolution, the Enlightenment, and the Romantic period; which promoted not only beauty, nature, and the imagination but the emotional spirit of freedom as well. Major reforms took place as a greater emphasis was placed on human rights, civility, reason, liberty, and respect for diversity. Consequently, the Paulines made the necessary adjustments in order to ensure their relevance; although, at the same time also doing everything they could to silence the rising voices of the modern age—such as confiscating the literary works of the luminary intellectuals of the Enlightenment (e.g., Voltaire; Rousseau; Diderot; etc.).[103]

Therefore, the Enlightenment and the modern-day world that we enjoy today, which places a greater value on human life, liberty, democracy, science, and ethics, did not arise because of Judeo-Christianity, but rather despite Judeo-Christianity.

* * *

The rediscovery of ancient Greek culture and ideas also helped to revive an interest in democracy. This rebirth helped to spark the historic revolutions that occurred in the eighteenth century. It was also during that time that an emphasis was placed on the need for the separation of church and state. This statute was intended to not only prevent a government from restricting personal liberty, and not only to prevent the infighting that was occurring between the Judeo-Christian denominations, but to prevent a leader from claiming some type of holy mandate that is above the common ethical standard and law of man—as Pauline rulers had done for centuries in the Old World. This safeguard was put into place because the humanists of the Enlightenment knew that when the affairs of church and state are intertwined, irrational and inhumane activities can be justified when the people are led to believe that there is a divine significance behind it. This is the situation behind the so-called "Holy War."

> Those who believe in absurdities will commit atrocities.
> —Voltaire, *Questions sur les miracles*

The humanistic principles that were advanced during the post Dark Age era is especially exemplified by the movements that occurred in the American New World. Although it is widely believed by many American Paulines that the United States of America was founded by Judeo-Christians, this is not entirely true. The laws of Jehovah actually contradict the original American values of liberty and democracy. Jehovah himself would have preferred a totalitarian theocracy. In fact, when Jehovah was on the Earth he actually embodied the persona of a Middle Eastern dictator with weapons of mass destruction!

American Paulines will sometimes cite the words "In God We Trust," which is the motto that is printed on federal property, in order to justify their position; however, this Judeo-Christian maxim is not the original motto of the United States. In fact, it did not even appear until almost a hundred years after the founding of the nation—although, even then it was used only on coinage. It did not become an officially recognized motto until 1956. The original motto that was used by the Founding Fathers was actually *E Pluribus Unum* (One Out of Many). Moreover, it does not say "In God We Trust" in the U.S. Constitution, but rather "We the People"; which is another reference to a democracy, not a theocracy.

American Paulines cite examples of the Founding Fathers referring to God and the principles of the Judeo-Christian faith; however, while it is true that many of the Founding Fathers of America did respect some of the basic principles of the Judeo-Christian religion—perhaps out of practical necessity—they were also students of philosophy and Enlightenment thinking. Some were also Deists, which included such prominent statesmen as Thomas Jefferson and Thomas Paine. Deism was a progressive Christian philosophy that embraced the value of reason over dogmatic faith. Some of the Founding Fathers, such as James Madison and Thomas Jefferson, even condemned traditional Judeo-Christianity as being corrupt.

> Paul was the [. . .] corrupter of the doctrines of Jesus.
> —Thomas Jefferson, Letter to William Short

> His [Jesus's] object was the reformation of some articles in

107

the religion of the Jews, as taught by Moses. That sect had presented for the object of their worship, a being of terrific[58] character, cruel, vindictive, capricious and unjust.
—Thomas Jefferson, Letter to William Short

Experience witnesseth that ecclesiastical establishments, instead of maintaining the purity and efficacy of religion, have had a contrary operation. During almost fifteen centuries has the legal establishment of Christianity been on trial. What has been its fruits? More or less, in all places, pride and indolence in the clergy; ignorance and servility in the laity; in both, superstition, bigotry and persecution. [. . .] What influence, in fact, have ecclesiastical establishments had on society? In some instances they have been seen to erect a spiritual tyranny on the ruins of the civil authority; on many instances they have been seen upholding the thrones of political tyranny; in no instance have they been the guardians of the liberties of the people. Rulers who wish to subvert the public liberty may have found an established clergy convenient auxiliaries. A just government, instituted to secure and perpetuate it, needs them not.
—James Madison, A Memorial and Remonstrance
(Addressed to the General Assembly of the Commonwealth of Virginia.)

The other influential group that was active during those years were the Freemasons, which included such esteemed members as Benjamin Franklin, John Hancock, Paul Revere, Andrew Jackson, and George Washington. The following passage is taken from a classic Masonic manuscript:

The two great motors are Truth and Love. When all these

---

58 Jefferson uses the word "terrific" here in the original sense of the word, which meant terrifying.

108

Forces are combined, and guided by the Intellect, and regulated by the Rule of Right, and Justice, and of combined and systematic movement and effort, the great revolution prepared for by the ages will begin to march.

—Albert Pike, *Morals and Dogma*

It is believed that the roots of Freemasonry can be traced back to mysterious "brotherhoods" (e.g., the Rosicrucians and the Knights Templar of the Middle Ages, etc.) who were thought to possess esoteric knowledge. This policy of secrecy has inspired many nefarious conspiracy theories over the years. Many present-day investigators who are influenced by the Pauline creed have linked these groups to a worldwide satanic conspiracy involving the antichrist, the so-called "New World Order," the Illuminati, and the apocalyptic end of the world.

Although its history may be open to debate, Freemasonry itself can only really be traced back to the stone-masons of the early European Renaissance period. It was originally a local trade fraternity. It was not until the early eighteenth century that some more inquisitive individuals began to delve into more esoteric topics. These more philosophical members were called "speculative," as opposed to "operative," Masons.

It is very likely that one of the reasons for all the secrecy had to do with the continuing threat that was posed by the officials of the Pauline institutions and the laity who they influenced. Indeed, the Paulines have had a tumultuous relationship with the esoteric brotherhoods over the centuries. Even though by the time the Freemasons arose the Inquisitions were coming to an end, the Paulines still had the ability to blacklist those who did not conform to its own tradition. Free-thinking and progressive ideas continued to be discouraged. Such condemnation and "excommunication" were enough to effect public reputations and careers. Indeed, many Freemasons were, and are, eminent public figures.

The reason for the secrecy does not have anything to do with a sinister plot, as is commonly believed, but rather with what was referred to by Jesus:

It is those who are worthy of my mysteries that I tell my

mysteries.

—Jesus, The Nag Hammadi Codices, The Gospel of Thomas

Do not give dogs what is sacred; do not throw your pearls to pigs. If you do, they may trample them under their feet, and turn and tear you to pieces.

—Jesus, Matthew 7:6

The unfortunate fact is that not everyone in the world is capable of understanding and accepting higher truths. Therefore, retaining special information may be necessary in some instances due to the imperfect condition of a world that is still in the midst of recovering from a less fortunate time. The truth is just about every informed individual hopes for the day when the truth can be made public to the entire world.

> Truth is not for those who are unworthy or unable to receive it, or would pervert it. The Teachers, even of Christianity, are, in general, the most ignorant of the true meaning of that which they teach. There is no book of which so little is known as the Bible.
>
> —Albert Pike, *Morals and Dogma*

Although it is debatable whether or not at least some of the Freemasons were (and are) aware of the difference between Yahweh/Jehovah and the heavenly Father of the universal Godhead[59] source, the official Masonic stance regarding the Supreme Being is that "The Great Architect of the Universe" is based upon one's own understanding of the Creator. This is why members of different faiths can all come together as fellow Masons.

Some present-day conspiratorialists believe that the Freemasons, along with the Bilderberger Group, the Trilateral Commission, the Council on Foreign Relations, as well as the mysterious Illuminati, are all scheming to create a tyrannical "one-world government" that will be

---

59 The Godhead is defined in this work as the original, transcendent, and supernatural life-force that pervades the living universe.

ruled over by the biblical antichrist. However, it should be understood that most of these theories are influenced by the mistaken precepts of the Pauline creed.

An inscription that is found on the U.S. dollar bill reads *Novus Ordo Seclorum*; however, this is not a reference to some sinister "New World Order," but rather to a "new order of the ages." This motto actually pertains to the new era that the great thinkers of that time were ushering in. The "great revolution prepared for by the ages" that was referred to by the Freemasons, as well as the New Order of the Ages that is printed on the U.S. dollar bill, actually have a much more benign meaning. After all, it was Masonic types who helped to pave the way for the great revolution that founded the free country of the United States of America, which became a modern-day model for freedom, prosperity, and democracy throughout the world.

Conspiracy theorists will undoubtedly counter this thesis by citing events in which some confirmed member of a "brotherhood organization" was exposed committing some unethical transgression. My response to that is that, statistically speaking, among any large group of people there are likely to be a minority who succumb to their shortcomings. However, I contend that burning down an entire orchard because of a few bad apples is both unnecessary and unwise.

Nevertheless, it must also be acknowledged that the presence of powerful special-interest groups and individuals who are actively pursuing an unethical agenda that would work to undermine democracy is indeed a realistic threat. However, in most cases these factions have more to do with the wealthy corporate elite (i.e., oligarchs/plutocrats) than with the defunct Illuminati. The primary aim of the wealthy corporate elite is to make money for themselves, which was not the primary aim of the esoteric brotherhoods. For example, the objective of the Illuminati was to oppose the dysfunctional dominance of Pauline Judeo-Christendom. What the Illuminati sought to establish in its place was a more humanistic regime that place a greater emphasis on secular philosophy and science. Therefore, the wealthy corporate elite and the so-called "brotherhood" organizations, such as the Illuminati, should not be conflated.

What the Founding Fathers of America established was not

specifically a Judeo-Christian nation, but rather a free and independent country that more highly regards personal liberty. The United States of America was founded upon the humanistic principle that all people should have the right to practice their religious beliefs, or not to at all, and not be persecuted one way or the other.

Proponents of the Pauline tradition, who believe that America was founded by Judeo-Christians, also often cite Paulines such as Christopher Columbus and the Puritans as examples; however, such people did not actually found the independent republic of the United States of America.

If there was no separation of church and state, various Pauline institutions might still be physically fighting for control of the government, since each of them would claim to know the-one-and-only "truth," and might even be willing to fight to the death in order to establish and preserve it. This is what the Founding Fathers were clearly hoping to prevent.

* * *

In the eighteenth century, a new Protestant movement began in Britain, and especially in the American colonies, that came to be referred to as the "Great Awakening." One of the primary instigators of that revival was Jonathan Edwards, a Calvinist preacher and theologian who was most known for his sermon "Sinners in the Hands of an Angry God."

In the early twentieth century, fundamentalism was officially reborn in America when sixty-four American and British preachers and theologians wrote a collection of essays titled *The Fundamentals*. This Old World Calvinist doctrine preceded the extremist "Christian Reconstructionism" movement, as well as other Old Testament-influenced ideologies that eschew science and higher forms of education, which they believe are being forced upon them by a corrupted secular materialist world. Consequently, an anti-intellectual backlash developed around the Puritanical flag of Old World tradition. The fundamentalists proceeded to establish their own academic institutions; institutions that not only asserted the mistaken Pauline interpretation but promoted a revisionist view of world history.

112

Many of these errors can be found in the present-day Evangelical movement.[60] Among other misconceptions, Evangelicals believe in the literal interpretation of the Bible; its absolute inerrancy; that salvation is attained through the death of the Christ (i.e., Substitionary Atonement/Crucicentrism), and that Jesus will return to Earth in a future Second Coming event. All of which are misinterpretations.

Many present-day Paulines cite tribulations in our own time, such as murder, drug use, sexual immorality, and the general decline in moral behavior, as signs of a fallen society that has strayed from God. However, it should be understood that just because a minority of individuals have not handled their freedom in a responsible manner does not mean that freedom or humanity itself is bad; nor is immorality something that is new to the human experience. Indeed, the actions of Yahweh and some of the Yahwehists themselves were what could be described as immoral.

The unfortunate and ironic reality is that if Jesus were to literally return, as many Paulines believe that he will, it is very likely that he would not conform to the stereotype that they have constructed of him; and it would be they themselves, like the Pharisees and the laity who they influenced before them, who would condemn him—most likely as "the antichrist"—and would seek to have him put to death. Despite significant progress in recent centuries, the unfortunate fact is that, in many cases, the primary mentality of the contentious and affected mind of the devoted Yahwehist has remained unchanged.

* * *

The Roman Pauline Papacy is the last of the ancient autocracies with a following larger than ever. Over one-billion people acknowledge the authority of the pope. Fortunately, the Catholic Church has taken some progressive steps in the past century. For example, despite objections by some in the Vatican council, Pope John Paul II apologized for the mistakes that were committed by members of the Catholic Church

---

60 There has been some debate whether the Evangelical movement can be equated with fundamentalism or not. After examination, I maintain that the two movements are indeed closely related.

through the centuries.[104] However, as long as "Jehovah" is continued to be misidentified as the heavenly Father of "Jesus," the very core foundation of this historic problem will continue to exist. In this case, the Paulines—including the Protestants—must not only acknowledge the dark side of their history but also the great misinterpretation that was committed by the early church patriarchs as well.

One of the success stories of the Pauline denominations in recent times, on the other hand, has been the commitment by its members to emphasize the beneficial power of the Holy Spirit, which is the energy of love, rejuvenation, and of healing. Unfortunately, this emotional truth can be used to mislead the faithful into believing the mistaken concepts that its leaders attach onto it.

CHAPTER III

EPILOGUE

It is commonly believed that subjects related to mind control and so-called "brain-washing" only apply to members of cults and totalitarian political regimes; however, this is not true. There are two basic types of mind control: direct and indirect. Direct cognitive manipulation pertains to victims who are forced into a situation in which they are overtly coerced into surrendering their mental autonomy (i.e., menticide) and adopting the beliefs of the dominating agent. Indirect mind control occurs on a subtle level. In these instances, the subject is not usually aware that the effect is occurring. Indirect thought reform can be accomplished through common sources: e.g., radio, television, books, etc. Through the use of these non-threatening everyday mediums, the agent asserts a particular conviction by presenting information that not only advances only one side of the issue, and not only presents their interpretations as irrefutable fact, and not only evokes emotional triggers, but uses fallacious disinformation to mislead their subjects. In a great majority of these instances, the agents themselves are not even aware that the information that they are asserting is either unethical and/or not true. This is because they themselves have been subjected to this very same conditioning. The most common aim of the dominating agent is to convince the subject to replace their own self interest with that of the agent and the institution that they are affiliated with.

The development and proliferation of false consciousness[61] also occurs in some conventional religious institutions. Those who resist are made to feel as if they are refusing "God's will." The price of disobeying the will of God is said to be eternal punishment in hell. The subject is also told that being a good person is not good enough, and that to make it into heaven one must become a devoted money-tithing, church leader-exalting, doctrine-adhering, member—and in some cases: soldier—of the organization.

The indoctrination process is most effective when it begins during childhood. When this occurs, the ideology becomes infused into the subject's fundamental cognitive orientation (i.e., *weltanschauung*).

> Common men find themselves inheriting their beliefs, they know not how.
> —William James,[62] *A Pluralistic Universe*

When confronted with the fact that this worldview is untrue many years later, the subject may be unable to come to terms with such an extreme schism. This type of cognitive dissonance upsets the comforts of the type of regulated normalcy that is represented in the Freudian concept of the super-ego. This resistance is especially salient when one's religious beliefs form the very bedrock of one's mores. When confronted with the facts, the subject may also be made to feel that the devil is trying to tempt them away from God. For others, the humiliation of having been misled is intolerable, and they will resist reform due to this reason alone. Similarly, others who have high opinions of themselves may also be under the impression that so-called "brain-washing" could never happen to them, and therefore resist reform due to an arrogant sense of certainty.

In some countries, most notably in the United States of America, the link between Pauline Judeo-Christianity, politics, big business, and the

---

61 This philosophical term is defined as a lack of awareness of the true source of one's beliefs. It can be related to *avidya*, which is the Hindu concept of ignorance, and *bi* (or *pi*), which is the Chinese Confucian term (from the philosopher Xunzi) for blindness of the mind.

62 William James was a nineteenth- and twentieth-century professor of philosophy and psychology at Harvard University.

military-industrial-congressional-complex[63] is especially consequential. Some at the top, who, in previous times were referred to as the "Robber Barons" and "the masters of mankind,"[64] and who are now more commonly referred to as plutocrats and oligarchs, have been able to use this conglomerate for their own advantage. Through the use of "think tanks," they have devised ways in which to not only foment an environment of moral skepticism (i.e., moral particularism)—especially in regard to honesty and avarice—but convince the general populace to replace their own self-interest, as well as the welfare of the environment, with that of the wealthy corporate elite. By disseminating disinformation (i.e., social constructivism) that exploit the fears, the prejudices, and the ignorance of the people, this faction has been able to take advantage of low-information voters—many of which themselves are abject members of the precariat.[65] Moreover, the plutocrats/oligarchs execute this reckless and unethical campaign while simultaneously aligning themselves with the cherished symbols of tradition (e.g, Bible; Constitution; flag; etc.) (i.e., the hyperreal simulation), which they use to conceal the sociopathic greed that underlies their patriotic pretense. This stratagem has been, for the most part, very effective.[66]

* * *

The contradictions, the duplicity, and the mistaken interpretations can finally be remedied by beginning with the fundamental fact that the heavenly Father of Jesus was not the Demiurge of the Old Testament.

Of course, the members of the institutions of Yahweh/Jehovah will adamantly fight to preserve the ways that they have become accustomed

---

63 The "military industrial complex" most often refers to the American military and the industry that supplies it. The term was popularized by President Dwight D. Eisenhower in his 1961 farewell address. In more recent times, the term has been extended to include the military industrial congressional complex, due to the role that politicians play in this operation.

64 From Adam Smith's book *Wealth of Nations* (1776).

65 The term "precariat" denotes the precarious state of the laborer class: i.e., the proletariat.

66 For more on this subject, I recommend the documentary *Requiem for the American Dream* (2016).

to.

> In short, the social, as opposed to the mystical function of a mythology, is not to open the mind, but to enclose it: to bind a local people together in mutual support by offering images that awaken the heart to recognitions of commonality, without allowing these to escape the monadic compound.
> —Joseph Campbell, *The Inner Reaches of Outer Space*

> New opinions are always suspected, and usually opposed, without any other reason but because they are not already common.
> —John Locke, *An Enquiry Concerning Human Understanding, Dedicatory Epistle*

Some hardened Paulines have even gone so far as to not only disparage the findings of science and the principles of the Enlightenment but even liberty and intellectualism itself. This type of behavior is exemplified in their condemnation of other belief systems, such as the present-day New Age movement; which many Paulines believe is related to sorcery, false gods, and the antichrist. However, according to Jesus himself the impostors will be exposed by their "fruit." The fruit of the New Age movement is peace, love, and enlightenment, which are the very same values that Jesus himself sought to encourage. The condemnation of movements that are related to peace, love, and enlightenment, is the residual influence imposed upon the world by the deceptive Lord of Armies.

It must be remembered that it was the Old World Paulines who also rejected the fact that the Earth orbits the sun. We have also seen this type of reaction manifested in our own time in their attack on the scientific theory of evolution. Proponents of creationism, under the vanguard banner of "intelligent design," will only accept scientific theories that they can use to bolster their ideology. However, it must be understood that the author of Genesis was not present during the creation of the world, and therefore used metaphorical descriptions in order to convey primary points. Scientific examination has revealed that our planet has developed over the course of billions of years. The author of the book of Genesis used the description of "days" in order to describe the different *stages* that the planet went through as it was formed. The description of days is, of course, not to be taken literally; just as the character of the serpent in the Garden of Eden story was not intended to represent a literal talking snake, but rather was intended to convey the description of a character who was thought to be dangerous.

Some Paulines have been using the "Junkyard Tornado" argument to support their claims about evolution (which is based on an example that was first proposed by the astronomer Fred Hoyle, and is related to the "watchmaker" analogy). According to this analogy, Darwin's theory of evolution is the equivalent of a tornado whirling up spare metal fragments in a junkyard into a fully-formed working 747 jet airplane. However, it must be understood that metal parts are not organic, and therefore do not adapt and mutate over the course of millennia the same way that biological organisms do. Therefore, this analogy does not disprove evolution, but rather only indicates that the Pauline opponents of science who are using this example do not understand biology.

The enlightened Christian should be open to a type of evolution that is influenced by the energy of the universal source, and should not reject the science of evolution altogether. In other words, it could be more accurately said that God (i.e., the Godhead of the heavenly Father) created evolution!

* * *

It is also necessary to clarify the Garden of Eden story by putting it into context with the findings. What must be understood is that the account that was described in the Old Testament/Tanakh is reported from the perspective of a follower of Yahweh/Jehovah, and therefore is incorrect. In other words, it was wrong for the Lord of Adam and Eve to deny his servants access to "life" and "knowledge"—i.e., the Tree of Life and the Tree of Knowledge of Good and Evil. This truth is referred to in the following gnostic Christian tractate:

> But what sort is this God? First he maliciously refused Adam from eating of the tree of knowledge, and, secondly, he said "Adam, where are you?" God does not have foreknowledge? Would he not know from the beginning? And afterwards, he said, "Let us cast him out of this place, lest he eat of the tree of life and live forever." Surely, he has shown himself to be a malicious grudger! And what kind of God is this? For great is the blindness of those who read, and they did not know him. And he said, "I am the jealous God; I will bring the sins of the fathers upon the children until three (and) four generations." And he said, "I will make their heart thick, and I will cause their mind to become blind, that they might not know nor comprehend the things that are said."
>
> —The Nag Hammadi Codices, The Testimony of Truth

The Old Testament record itself informs us that the so-called "serpent" character did not actually intend to harm Adam and Eve, but rather had compassion for human-beings who had been forced to live life as nothing more than lowly servants in a so-called "garden." However, it must be understood that the garden was not some heavenly realm of recreation and relaxation. The record tells us that the Lord put Adam in the garden to work in it (Genesis 2:15), not to enjoy a permanent holiday in paradise. Therefore, what was referred to as a garden was actually a farm on the steppe plains of the Sumerian *Edinnu* (i.e., Eden). The truth is that it was only a relaxing paradise for "God" himself.

The description of the serpent as the devil is also incorrect. This was actually a hypocritical accusation that was made by the agents of the jealous and deceptive Lord of Armies. The truth is that this individual who was compared to a snake was actually compassionate toward human-beings, and sought to lift them from out of an oppressive system that had made them into nothing more than workers and worshipers. (The warriors of the Lord of Armies came later.) Indeed, in the biblical record

120

itself references to the beneficial symbol of snake can be found:

[. . .] Therefore be wise as serpents [. . .]
—Jesus, Matthew 10:16

Just as Moses lifted up the serpent in the wilderness, so the
Son of Man must also be lifted up.
—Jesus, John 3:14

Of course, it was easy for the agents of Yahweh/Jehovah to turn this
symbol into something hideous and intimidating, even though this is not
the original connotation.

One of the gnostic Christian groups that were active in the early years
were what has come to be known as the Naassenes. This designation was
applied to this group by one of its proto-orthodox detractors,
Hippolytus.[105] According to this third-century Pauline theologian,[67] the
Naasenes were a heretical faction that celebrated the serpent. Hippolytus
derived the name from the word *naas*, which he believed was the Hebrew
word for serpent (i.e., *nehash/nachash*). This group may be related to, or
are the same group who are known as, the Ophites—which derives from
the Greek word *ophis*, which also means serpent.[106]

Likewise, the character of so-called "Lucifer" is also based on yet
another misinterpretation. The name Lucifer is derived from the Latin
words *lux/lucis* (light), and *ferre* (bring, or to bear), which can be
translated as "light-bearer," "morning star," "day star," or "shining one."
It is a designation that is influenced by the following passage:

O how you have fallen from heaven, you shining one
[lucifer], son of the dawn! How you have been cut down to
the earth, you who were disabling the nations.
—Isaiah 14:12

However, what is not commonly understood about this passage is that it
does not actually refer to the devil. At the beginning of this proverb

---

67 Refutation of All Heresies (Book V)

(Isaiah 14:4), it is reported that this particular taunt was directed at "the king of Babylon." This is who the "son of the dawn" originally referred to. Therefore, the word that is sometimes translated as "Lucifer" (from the original Hebrew word *he lel*) was not originally a name. The author was actually conveying the point that although the king may have once been as glorious as the morning star, his shinning splendor had been brought to an end. It was during a later time that the character of Lucifer as a fallen light-bearer, who was the one-and-only devil, developed. This deviation did not occur until the New Testament era (2 Corinthians 11:14), where Satan is described as an "angel of light" (*aggelon photos*), who was seen falling "like lightning from heaven" (Luke 10:18); which was most likely a based on a misinterpretation of the Isaiah text.

* * *

Another step that must be taken in the reformation of the Catholic Church is the abolition of institutionalized clerical celibacy. This obligational rejection of sexuality that the priests of the Roman Catholic Church (and Eastern Orthodox Church) have been led to practice has led to widespread dysfunction; a dysfunction which has manifested itself in the form of the perversion of pedophilia. This is very likely one of the results of the misdirected libido when it is unnaturally repressed. Celibacy can be a great way of establishing independence and emotional stability. However, this decision must be a personal one; not the life-long result of an institutional decree.

In regard to the child abuse cases, investigations have revealed that priests who engaged in pedophilia was far more widespread than had been previously thought. The official estimate (according to the John Jay report)[68] of the total number of cases involving pedophiliac priest is 4,392, and the number of children who were abused is 10,667! In many cases, even after officials in the Catholic Church were made aware of the allegations law enforcement investigators were never contacted, and the

---

68 The John Jay Report, or "The Nature and Scope of the Problem of Sexual Abuse of Minors by Catholic Priests and Deacons in the United States," is a 2004 study commissioned by the U.S. Conference of Catholic Bishops that was conducted by the John Jay College of Criminal Justice.

offenders were instead transferred to other parishes where the abuse continued.[107] In some cases, compensation payments were made on the condition that the victims remain silent.[108] Investigations revealed that church leaders had not done enough to stop the abuse.[109] This is apparently because there were some who believed that the welfare of the Catholic Church superseded that of the children.

Dysfunctional behavior related to sexuality and Pauline denomination misunderstandings is also exemplified in the "God Hates Fags" movement of the Kansas Westboro Baptist Church. The excuse that is used to justify this policy of intolerance toward homosexuals is based not only on the New Testament letters of Paul (Romans 1:26; 1 Corinthians 6:9) but from Jehovah himself. The reference is found in Leviticus 18:22, in which it is reported that Jehovah considered homosexuality to be an "abomination." Jesus himself did not directly comment on this issue (that we know of); however, we can draw a conclusion based on the actions and teachings of Jesus himself, that he would have not shared the same hostile and narrow-minded mentality that Jehovah and Paul did. In fact, in the very same book of the Bible Jehovah not only ordered a blasphemer to be stoned to death (Leviticus 24:23) but affirmed the law "an eye for an eye, a tooth for a tooth" (Leviticus 24:19); both of which are practices that Jesus directly overturned! (Matthew 5:38; John 8:7) Also, in the very same book Jehovah decreed that his followers must not cut the hair at the sides of their head, nor could they trim the edges of their beard (Leviticus 19:27), nor could they "wear clothing woven of two kinds of material," nor were they allowed to plant their fields with "two kinds of seed" (Leviticus 19:19). They were also instructed not to eat pigs (which would include bacon and ham) and seafood that does not have "fins and scales," such as crabs and lobsters (Leviticus 11:7-10). In this case, one must wonder how many hardened Pauline zealots who are discriminating against homosexual people are guilty of committing such erroneous transgressions. Furthermore, according to the very same book of the Old Testament, slavery was permitted! (Leviticus 25:44)

Fundamentalist Paulines also cite Matthew 5:17, in which Jesus appears to affirm the regulations of the Old Testament; however, as was previously noted, the Gospel of Matthew is the least accurate of the accounts. Indeed, this passage contradicts the actions of Jesus elsewhere in the gospels, where it is reported that he endeavored to nullify Old Testament thinking. Therefore this passage, which only appears in the Gospel of Matthew, and does not appear in the more authentic source material, such as Mark and Q, cannot be considered to be an accurate representation of what he actually said.

Another passage that is cited by the Paulines is the following:

> Some pharisees came to him to test him. They asked, "Is it lawful for a man to divorce his wife for any and every reason?" "Haven't you read," he replied, "that at the beginning the Creator 'made them male and female,' and said, 'For this reason a man will leave his father and mother and be united to his wife, and the two will become one flesh'? So they are no longer two, but one flesh. Therefore what God has joined together, let no one separate."
> —Matthew 19:3-6

However, in this passage Jesus is actually only referring to the issue of divorce and the institution of marriage itself. The words "man" and "women" were used only because that is the most common form of marriage, not because he was making a statement about homosexuality. Indeed, homosexuality is never specifically mentioned in the gospels. Therefore, the relationship between "sexual immorality" (Matthew 15:19) and homosexuality is only a forced conflation.

It is also disingenuous to cite the words of Paul to support an anti homosexual argument; not only because of the previously cited discrepancies between the teachings of Paul and Jesus but because Paul himself stated that Old Testament law was no longer required for salvation! (Romans 7:6, 6:24; 2 Corinthians 3:14; Galatians 2:16, 3:13, 23-25, 2:21, 5:4) Furthermore, according to Paul's own interpretation the people will not be saved by the old covenant but by the "new covenant" (2 Corinthians 3:6, 3:14), which simply required "faith" in Christ (Galatians 3:11). Therefore, when Paul is condemning homosexuality he is actually contradicting himself!

The enlightened viewpoint of this issue is that the discrimination, the persecution, the hatred, and the violence that is being directed at homosexuals is the real sin. This is the type of blasphemy against the Holy Spirit that the Savior warned about (Mark 3:29). Consenting adults who engage in intimate and loving relationships are not evil. The real issue has to do with the problem of mental conditioning that results in bigotry, hatred, and in some cases, even violence.

* * *

Throughout this book the word "enlightenment" has been referred to. What is enlightenment? How can it be defined?

According to the eighteenth-century German philosopher Immanuel Kant, enlightenment is the successful emergence of an individual from out of a state of mental "immaturity." Kant believed that this state of immaturity is the result of cowardice and mental laziness—I would also add arrogance. He proposed that the enlightened individual, on the other hand, is a bold and free-spirited type of person. A person who dares to be wise.

In ancient India, enlightenment was described in comparable but slightly different terms. Although the higher state of consciousness that was attained by the Buddha is commonly translated as "enlightenment," a more accurate rendering is "awakened" (*bodhi*). To be awakened is to understand the true nature of things, which in turn leads to liberation (*moksha*) from the suffering that is caused by delusion.

It would seem that enlightenment can be defined as both a state of clarity as well as a state of awareness. The clarity aspect refers to the realization of the difference between the artificial Demiurge/man-made world and its related military, industrial, religious, economic, and political perspectives (i.e., the hyperreal simulation),[69] and the natural world.

---

69 For more on this subject, see: *Simulacra and Simulation* by Jean Baudrillard. University of Michigan Press, 1994.

Follow Nature! Follow Nature! As she works so will I work!

—Rosicrucian Motto[70]

The awareness aspect may refer to educational knowledge; although it might also relate to spiritual awareness. This may pertain to the realization that there is more occurring in this world than our standard everyday work and material-based experience would influence us to believe. It is possible that the mystical adept (e.g., Yeshua the Savior) is one who is able to attune to a higher level of consciousness, in which the realm of supernatural energy is experienced. However, mental enlightenment may not always be coincident with spiritual awareness and virtue. Indeed, there is a physical life, a mental life, and a spiritual life. Spiritual enlightenment, as opposed to mental enlightenment, may refer not only to spiritual awareness but to internal rectification. This may relate to the meditative process by which one removes his or herself from the maladies that might cause one to deviate from a more life-supporting ethical standard. To live the spiritually enlightened way is to be personally empowered, without being narcissistic, and to see one's self as being connected and in peaceful harmony with the "way" (i.e., the *Tao*) of the natural spirit of the universe.

Some people may choose not to embrace the belief in the divinity of one's self, and instead may turn to the aid of a protective and inspirational religious figure, which can also be beneficial—that is, as long as those instructing individuals do not abuse their positions.

People who have achieved both mental and spiritual enlightenment have conquered issues, such as fear and hatred, by not only establishing a strong personal connection with the divine but by understanding and feeling compassion for those who do not. Indeed, many people are stuck in negative habit cycles because no one has helped to guide them from out of the ignorant and hostile world that they have been effected by.

However, an enlightened adept also knows when strength and confrontation is necessary. Yeshua knew that there were times to both

---

70 Schrodter, Willy. *A Rosicrucian Notebook: The Secret Sciences Used by Members of the Order.* Weiser Books, 1992.

126

"turn the other cheek"—in order to maintain the moral high ground and to appeal to the antagonist's intrinsic ethical nature—and to stand up and challenge the ignorant, the arrogant, and the malicious, in an honorable manner.

There are indeed living beings who can be considered to be "angels," but they do not wear robes or have wings, and their halos are not commonly visible. Indeed, they are unassuming everyday people who do not seek to fit into the stereotypes of man.

* * *

When the intelligent, enlightened, peaceful, and ethical mentality is more regarded than the domineering ways of the selfish, the hateful, the ignorant, the fearful, and the arrogantly close-minded, the world will move a little more closer to a Heaven on Earth—which should be the ultimate paragon goal of every virtuous human-being.

Of course, many of those who are still effected by the past will seek to suppress such an ideal. Such hard-hearted and mentally-affected individuals are bound to preserve the institutions that not only have they become accustomed to, or that they have been influenced to preserve, but that they have been able to derive some kind of personal benefit from as well. Of course, these types of benefits usually manifest in the political and economic world as some type of materialistic form of prosperity. In the present-day world, the problem of greed, deceit, ignorance, arrogance, corruption, sociopathic malice, and the lust for power, wealth, and fame, is just as prevalent as it was in biblical times. This is the same type of immature and destructive behavior that fueled the internal fire of the wicked god of war. Indeed, this is the same type of iniquity that Yeshua spoke out against (Mark 7:22).

The traditional practice of white-washing the abominations of Yahweh/Jehovah must also be brought to an end. The cover-up of the atrocities that were committed by the Machiavellian Lord of Armies and his associates continues to this very day by devoted priests, reverends, rabbis, etc., who often tell the people what they want to hear, instead of what is actually documented in the Bible itself.

Due to the influence of not only pious sermons but Renaissance artworks and Hollywood movies, the world has been effected by a magical view of the biblical past. This artificial projection has unfortunately caused even further confusion. The truth is that before this modern age life was primitive and harsh, and before this Age of Information that we enjoy today, legitimate information was not as available. The truth is that the fantastical Golden Age that many who are immersed in the Judeo-Christian tradition believe happened, never actually happened.

It should also be understood that just because an institution is large, or an interpretation is old, does not mean that it is correct. The fact is that the time for discovering and understanding the truth is not in the primitive past, but now. Indeed, just because some choose not to believe in the reality of evolution does not mean that it is not actually happening.

The unfortunate fact is that many people, if not most, are not sincere seekers of the truth. Such people adhere to beliefs that either they themselves feel the most comfortable with, or that others have imposed upon them. For many, the shock that the belief system that has been instilled into them since childhood is incorrect will be too much to bear, and they will resist change due to this reason alone. Nevertheless, the truth must be made available to those who are ready to receive it.

Those who are influenced by mistaken Pauline interpretations often use the threat of an antichrist or devil figure to frighten the laity away from progress and back toward the superficial comfort of established doctrine. Although, in regard to such a deceptive character, it must be understood that when people become informed they become empowered, and when they become empowered they are less likely to be misled by "Almighty" "Lord" or "Master" types. Indeed, the enlightened individual is more likely to be inspired by the least expected of life's little miracles. This is the principle that Jesus himself promoted when he said that the very least among us will be the greatest in heaven (Luke 9:48).

Of course, this epic story is far from over; rather, this post-apocalyptic age is still developing. Indeed, Yeshua knew that the historic revolution that he initiated would not occur in only a single generation. Instead, he stated that his teachings were like a seed that would one day sprout and flourish; and it is under this same type of hopeful spirit that this work is submitted.

> Then you will know the truth, and the truth will set you free.
> —Yeshua, John 8:32

NOTES

1. Phillip E. Goble, *The Orthodox Jewish Bible* (Afi International Publishers, 2002), 1168.

2. Bart D. Ehrman, *Jesus Interrupted: Revealing the Hidden Contradictions in the Bible: and Why We Don't Know About Them* (Harper One, 2009), 32.
. Michael Grant, *Herod the Great* (American Heritage Press, 1971), 229.

3. Uri Yosef, "Who is the Suffering Servant in 'Isaiah 53?': Part I - The Jewish Interpretation: Valid or Not?" The Messiah Truth Project (2001-2011): 1-2. http://thejewishhome.org/counter/Isa53CP.pdf

4. Bart D. Ehrman, *Misquoting Jesus: The Story Behind Who Changed the Bible and Why* (Harper One, 2005), 64.

5. Bart D. Ehrman, *Jesus Interrupted: Revealing the Hidden Contradictions in the Bible (and Why We Don't Know About Them)* (Harper One, 2009), 153.
. Daniel J. Harrington, *The Gospel of Matthew* (Liturgical Press, 1991), 6.

6. Delbert Burkett, *An Introduction to the New Testament and the Origins of Christianity* (Cambridge University Press, 2002), 121, 156.
. Bart D. Ehrman, *Jesus Interrupted: Revealing the Hidden Contradictions in the Bible (and Why We Don't Know About Them)* (Harper One, 2009), 109, 112.

7. Delbert Burkett, *An Introduction to the New Testament and the Origins of Christianity* (Cambridge University Press, 2002), 156-157.
. Bart D. Ehrman, *Jesus Interrupted: Revealing the Hidden Contradictions in the Bible (and Why We Don't Know About Them)* (Harper One, 2009), 112.

8. Bart D. Ehrman, *Jesus Interrupted: Revealing the Hidden Contradictions in the Bible (and Why We Don't Know About Them)* (Harper One, 2009), 153.
. Burton L Mack, *The Lost Gospel: The Book of Q and Christian Origins* (Harper, 1993), 4.

9. Daniel J. Harrington, *The Gospel of Matthew* (Liturgical Press, 1991), 8.

10. Willis Barnstone, ed., *The Other Bible: Ancient Alternative Scriptures* (Harper, 1984), 517.
. Karel van der Toorn. *Scribal Culture: and the Making of the Hebrew Bible.*

(Harvard University Press, 2007), 28.

11. Daniel J. Harrington, *The Gospel of Matthew* (Liturgical Press, 1991), 8.

12. Daniel J. Harrington, *The Gospel of Matthew* (Liturgical Press, 1991), 9.
. John Nolland, *The Gospel of Matthew: A Commentary on the Greek Text* (Eerdmans, 2005), 18.

13. Bart D. Ehrman, *Misquoting Jesus: The Story Behind Who Changed the Bible and Why* (Harper One, 2005), 10.

14. Bart D. Ehrman, *Lost Christianities: The Battles for Scripture and the Faiths We Never Knew.* (Oxford University Press, 2003), 109.

15. Richard Valantasis, *The Gospel of Thomas* (Routledge, 1997), 9.

16. Bart D. Ehrman, *Misquoting Jesus: The Story Behind Who Changed the Bible and Why* (Harper One, 2005), 26.

17. Rodolphe Kasser, ed., et al., *The Gospel of Judas: from Codex Tchacos* (National Geographic Society 2006), 37.

18. Ithamar Gruenwald, *Apocalyptic and Merkavah Mysticism*: 2nd rev. ed. (Brill, 2014), 113.

19. James M. Robinson, ed., *The Nag Hammadi Library in English* (Harper, 1988). [reprint: 4th ed. (Brill, 1996)], 29-30.

20. Bart D. Ehrman, *Lost Christianities: The Battles for Scripture and the Faiths We Never Knew* (Oxford University Press, 2003), 111-112.

21. Catherine A. Cory, *The Book of Revelation: New Collegeville Bible Commentary* (Liturgical Press, 2006), 7.

22. Bart D. Ehrman, *Forged: Writing in the Name of God – Why the Bible's Authors Are Not Who They Think They Are* (Harper One, 2011), 21.

23. Stephan A. Hoeller, *Gnosticism: New Light on the Ancient Tradition of Inner Knowing* (Quest Books, 2002), 98-99.
. Wilhem Schneemelcher, *The New Testament Apocrypha: Volume Two: Writings Related to the Apostles; Apocalypses and Related Subjects.* rev. ed. (James Clarke & Co. Ltd. and Westminster/John Knox Press, 1989 [English translation 1992]),

87.

24. Elaine Pagels, *Revelations: Visions, Prophecy, & Politics in the Book of Revelation* (Viking, 2012), 135, 144-149. 160.

25. Catherine A. Cory, *The Book of Revelation,* New Collegeville Bible Commentary (Liturgical Press, 2006), 76.
. Bart D. Ehrman, *Jesus Interrupted: Revealing the Hidden Contradictions in the Bible (and Why We Don't Know About Them)* (Harper One, 2009), 98.
. Michael L. White, "Understanding the Book of Revelation." PBS.org/Frontline (1999), accessed May 9, 2013.
http://www.pbs.org/wgbh/pages/frontline/shows/apocalypse/revelation/white.html

26. Michael L. White, "Understanding the Book of Revelation." PBS.org/Frontline (1999), accessed May 9, 2013.
http://www.pbs.org/wgbh/pages/frontline/shows/apocalypse/revelation/white.html

27. Steven J. Friesen, *Imperial Cults and the Apocalypse of John: Reading Revelation in the Ruins* (Oxford University Press, 2001), 46, 60.
. Michael L. White, "Understanding the Book of Revelation." PBS.org/Frontline (1999), accessed May 9, 2013.
http://www.pbs.org/wgbh/pages/frontline/shows/apocalypse/revelation/white.html

28. Michael L. White, "Understanding the Book of Revelation." PBS.org/Frontline (1999), accessed May 9, 2013.
http://www.pbs.org/wgbh/pages/frontline/shows/apocalypse/revelation/white.html

29. Catherine A.Cory, *The Book of Revelation,* New Collegeville Bible Commentary (Liturgical Press, 2006), 61.
. Elaine Pagels, *Revelations: Visions, Prophecy, & Politics in the Book of Revelation* (Viking, 2012), 33.

30. Elaine Pagels, *Revelations: Visions, Prophecy, & Politics in the Book of Revelation* (Viking, 2012), 32-33.
. Michael L. White, "Understanding the Book of Revelation." PBS.org/Frontline (1999), accessed May 9, 2013.
http://www.pbs.org/wgbh/pages/frontline/shows/apocalypse/revelation/white.html

31. Christopher Kelly, *The End of Empire: Attila the Hun & the Fall of Rome* (W.W. Norton & Co.), 2010.), 102, 115.
. Jacques Le Goff, *Medieval Civilization* (Blackwell Publishing, 1991), 14.
. James J. O'Donnell, *The Ruin of the Roman Empire: A New History* (Ecco,

2009), 91.

32. Jacques Le Goff, *Medieval Civilization* (Blackwell Publishing, 1991), 14.
. Herwing Wolfram, *The Roman Empire and Its Germanic Peoples* (University of California Press, 1997), 76.

33. Haig Bosmajian, *Burning Books* (McFarland, 2006), 38.

34. Holbrook Jackson, *The Anatomy of Bibliomania* (University of Illinois Press, 2001), 407.

35. William Barry, "Arius," *The Catholic Encyclopedia*, Vol. 1 (Robert Appleton Co., 1907), accessed March 17, 2015.
http://www.newadvent.org/cathen/01718a.htm
. Haig Bosmajian, *Burning Books* (McFarland, 2006), 38-39.

36. Duncan McMillan et al., *Société Rencesvals, Guillaume d'Orange and the chanson de geste: essays presented to Duncan McMillan in celebration of his seventieth birthday by his friends and colleagues of the Société Rencesvals* (University of Reading, 1984), 137.

37. Haig Bosmajian, *Burning Books* (McFarland, 2006), 52.

38. Mary K. Miller, "Reading Between the Lines: Scientists with High-Tech Tools are Deciphering Lost Writings of the Ancient Greek Mathematician Archimedes," *Smithsonian Magazine* (2007), accessed May 5, 2015.
http://www.smithsonianmag.com/science-nature/reading-between-the-lines-148131057/

39. Haig Bosmajian, *Burning Books* (McFarland, 2006), 44-46.

40. Gotthard Victor Lechler, *John Wycliffe and his English Precursors* (The Religious Tract Society, 1904), 502.

41. Haig Bosmajian, *Burning Books* (McFarland, 2006), 63.
. Bill Cooke, *Dictionary of Atheism, Skepticism, and Humanism* (Prometheus Books, 2006), 499.

42. Robert Irwin, *The Alhambra* (Profile Books, 2005), 95.

43. Haig Bosmajian, *Burning Books* (McFarland, 2006), 28.

44. Ibid.,105-106, 128.

45. Ibid., 28.

46. Martin Luther, *Three Treatises: From the American Edition of Luther's Works,* 2nd rev. ed. (Fortress Press, 1970), 225.

47. Haig Bosmajian, *Burning Books* (McFarland, 2006), 88.
. Barbara Sher Tinsley, *Pierre Bayle's Reformation: Conscience and Criticism on the Eve of the Enlightenment* (Susquehanna University Press, 2001), 289.

48. Haig Bosmajian, *Burning Books* (McFarland, 2006), 9, 53, 77, 84.

49. Ibid., 77-78.

50. Ibid., 68.

51. Henry Kamen, *The Spanish Inquisition: A Historical Revision* (Yale University Press, 1999), 104-105.

52. Haig Bosmajian, *Burning Books* (McFarland, 2006), 93.

53. Ibid., 66.

54. Ibid., 8-9.

55. Ibid., 56.

56. Mary K. Miller, "Reading Between the Lines: Scientists with High-Tech Tools are Deciphering Lost Writings of the Ancient Greek Mathematician Archimedes," *Smithsonianmag.com* (Mar 2007), accessed Jan 2, 2015.
http://www.smithsonianmag.com/science-nature/reading-between-the-lines-148131057/

57. Haig Bosmajian, *Burning Books* (McFarland, 2006), 73-74.

58. Bart D. Ehrman, *Misquoting Jesus: The Story Behind Who Changed the Bible and Why* (Harper One, 2005), 209.

59. Johnathan Phillips, *The Crusades: 1095-1197.* 2nd ed. (Routledge, 2014), 35, 71, 166, 181.
. Johnathan Riley Smith, *The Crusades: A History* (Yale University Press, 2005),

133-134.

60. Karen Armstrong, *Holy War: The Crusades and Their Impact on Today's World* (Doubleday, 1988), 386.

61. Karen Armstrong, *Holy War: The Crusades and Their Impact on Today's World* (Doubleday, 1988), 387.
. Johnathan Phillips, *The Crusades: 1095-1197.* 2nd ed. (Routledge, 2014), 144, 147, 166.

62. Wendy Doniger, *Merriam-Webster's Encyclopedia of World Religions* (Merriam-Webster, 1999), 1012.

63. Charles Freeman, *The Closing of the Western Mind: The Rise of Faith and the Fall of Reason* (Alfred A. Knopf, 2003), 320-321.

64. Ibid., 309-311.

65. Encyclopedia Britannica, s.v. "Michael Servetus," accessed Jan 21, 2015. http://www.britannica.com/EBchecked/topic/535958/Michael-Servetus

66. World Book Encyclopedia, H. Vol. 9, s.v. "Hospital," (World Book, A. Scott Fetzer Company, 2015).

67. Ravi P. Rannan-Eliya and Nishan De Mel, "Resource Mobilization in Sri Lanka's Health Sector," Department of Population & International Health, Harvard School of Public Health & Health Policy Programme, Institute of Policy Studies, hsph.harvard.edu (1997): 19, accessed Dec 28, 2014. https://www.hsph.harvard.edu/ihsg/publications/pdf/No-42.PDF

68. *Encyclopedia Britannica Online*, s.v. "Ebers Papyrus," accessed Jan 10, 2016. http://www.britannica.com/topic/Ebers-papyrus

69. *Encyclopedia Britannica Online*, s.v. "Edwin Smith Papyrus," accessed Jan 10, 2016. http://www.britannica.com/topic/Edwin-Smith-papyrus

70. Samuel Noah Kramer, *History Begins at Sumer: Thirty-Nine Firsts in Man's Recorded History.* 3rd ed. (University Press, 1981), 60-63.

71. Haig Bosmajian, *Burning Books* (McFarland, 2006), 45.

72. Marvin Perry et al., *Western Civilization: Ideas, Politics, and Society.* 9th ed.

(Houghton Mifflin Harcourt Publishing Co., 2008), 263.

.Paul Vincent Spade et al., "Medieval Philosophy," Edward N. Zalta, ed., The *Stanford Encyclopedia of Philosophy*, Plato.stanford.edu., (2013), accessed Jan 22, 2015. http://plato.stanford.edu/entries/medieval-philosophy/

73. Paul Vincent Spade et al., "Medieval Philosophy," Edward N. Zalta, ed., The *Stanford Encyclopedia of Philosophy*, Plato.stanford.edu., (2013), accessed Jan 22, 2015. http://plato.stanford.edu/entries/medieval-philosophy/

74. Ibid.

75. Hans Thijssen, "Condemnation of 1277," Edward N. Zalta, ed., The *Stanford Encyclopedia of Philosophy*, Plato.stanford.edu. (2013), accessed Jan 23, 2015. http://plato.stanford.edu/entries/condemnation/

76. Rivka Feldhay, *Galileo and the Church* (Cambridge University Press, 1995), 205-207.

77. Edward Rosen, *Copernicus and his Successors*, Erna Hilfstein, ed. (Hambledon Press, 1995), 198.

78. Ibid., 166-167.

79. Johann Peter Kirsch, "Stedingers," *The Catholic Encyclopedia*. Vol. 14 (New York: Robert Appleton Co., 1912), accessed April 24, 2015. http://www.newadvent.org/cathen/14283c.htm

80. Leon Poliakov, *The History of Anti-Semitism,* Vol. 2. (University of Pennsylvania, 2003), 156-157.

81. J. Arendzen, "Manichaenism," *The Catholic Encyclopedia,* Vol. 9 (Appleton Co., *Newadvent.org*, 1910), accessed Feb-2-2015. http://www.newadvent.org/cathen/09591a.htm

82. Ibid.

83. Cecil Roth, *The Spanish Inquisition* (W.W. Norton & Co., 1996), 21, 274.

84. Edwards Peters, *Torture* (Basil Blackwell, 1985), 65.

85. Jonathan Kirsch, *The Grand Inquisitor's Manual: A History of Terror in the Name of God* (Harper One, 2008), 105-106.

. Edwards Peters, *Torture* (Basil Blackwell, 1985), 68, 167.

86. Jonathan Kirsch, *The Grand Inquisitor's Manual: A History of Terror in the Name of God* (Harper One, 2008), 104-105.
. Edwards Peters, *Torture* (Basil Blackwell, 1985), 167.

87. Jonathan Kirsch, *The Grand Inquisitor's Manual: A History of Terror in the Name of God* (Harper One, 2008), 106.
. Edwards Peters, *Torture* (Basil Blackwell, 1985), 68, 167.

88. Jonathan Kirsch, *The Grand Inquisitor's Manual: A History of Terror in the Name of God* (Harper One, 2008),105.

89. Joseph Blotzer, "Inquisition," *The Catholic Encyclopedia*, Vol. 8 (Robert Appleton Co., 1910), accessed July 16, 2015.
http://www.newadvent.org/cathen/08026a.htm

90. Jonathan Kirsch, *The Grand Inquisitor's Manual: A History of Terror in the Name of God* (Harper One, 2008), 16, 111.
. Edwards Peters, *Torture* (Basil Blackwell, 1985), 69.

91. Jonathan Kirsch, *The Grand Inquisitor's Manual: A History of Terror in the Name of God* (Harper One, 2008), 76.

92. Ibid., 109.

93. Ibid., 108.

94. Ibid., 120.

95. Ibid., 103.

96. Brian P. Levack, *The Witch Hunt in Early Modern Europe,* 3rd ed. (Longman, 2006), 23.

97. Walter Nigg, *The Heretics: Heresy Through the Ages* (Dorset Press, 1990), 190.

98. Mark U. Edwards, *Luther and the False Brethren* (Stanford University Press, 1975), 66.

99. Walter Nigg, *The Heretics: Heresy Through the Ages* (Dorset Press, 1990), 304.

100. Haig Bosmajian, *Burning Books* (McFarland, 2006): 88, 95.

101. *Encyclopedia Britannica Online*, s.v. "History of Europe," accessed Jan 27, 2015. http://www.britannica.com/EBchecked/topic/195896/history-of-Europe

102. John T. Paoletti and Gary M. Radke, *Art in Renaissance Italy,* 3rd ed. (Laurence King Publishing, 2005), 27, 51.

103. Haig Bosmajian, *Burning Books* (McFarland, 2006), 118.

104. Rory Caroll, "Pope says sorry for sins of church," Theguardian.com (Mar 13, 2000), accessed Jan 2, 2015. http://www.theguardian.com/world/2000/mar/13/catholicism.religion

105. Mark H.Gaffney, *Gnostic Secrets of the Naassenes: The Initiatory Teachings of the Last Supper* (Inner Traditions, 2004), 6.

106. Ibid., 6.

107. Robin E. Clark and Judith Freeman Clark, *The Encyclopedia of Child Abuse,* 3rd ed. (Facts on File, 2007), 78.

108. Walter V. Robinson et al., "Scores of Priests Involved in Sex Abuse Cases: Settlements Kept Scope of Issue Out of Public Eye," *Boston.com* (Jan 31, 2002), accessed Jan 15, 2015. http://www.boston.com/globe/spotlight/abuse/stories/013102_priests.htm

109. Laurie Goodstein, Nick Cumming-Bruce, and Jim Yardley, "U.N. Panel Criticizes the Vatican Over Sexual Abuse," *Nytimes.com* (Feb 5, 2014), accessed Jan 17, 2015. http://www.nytimes.com/2014/02/06/world/europe/un-panel-assails-vatican-over-sex-abuse-by-priests.html?_r=0

ADDITIONAL INTERNET SOURCES:

www.biblegateway.com/

www.catholic.org/encyclopedia

gnosis.org/

www.gutenberg.org

legacy.fordham.edu/

lexiconcordance.com/

www.newadvent.org/

plato.stanford.edu

www.sacred-texts.com/

www.scripture4all.org/

ABOUT THE AUTHOR

I am a former associate member and contributing writer for The Center for Progressive Christianity (progressivechristianity.org). My articles have appeared in the Consortiumnews.com, Spiritualityandcommunity.com, and the Esoteric Christianity E-Magazine. I am also former member of the Church of Christ and former featured blogger at Crossleft.com. I am currently blogging on my website, aerikvondenburg.com.

www.ingramcontent.com/pod-product-compliance
Lightning Source LLC
LaVergne TN
LVHW051126080426
835510LV00018B/2257